MW00768382

SILVER THREADS & GOLDEN WISDOM

Daily Moments with the Master

GEORGE C. MOORE

The quoted ideas expressed in this book (but not scripture verses) are not, in all cases, exact quotations, as some have been edited for clarity and brevity. In all cases, the author has attempted to maintain the speaker's original intent. In some cases, quoted material for this book was obtained from secondary sources, primarily print media. While every effort was made to ensure the accuracy of these sources, the accuracy cannot be guaranteed. For additions, deletions, corrections or clarifications in future editions of this text, please write ELM HILL BOOKS.

For additions, deletions, corrections, or clarifications in future editions of this text, please contact Paul Shepherd, Executive Director for Elm Hill Books. Email pshepherd@elmhillbooks.com.

All Scripture quotations unless otherwise marked are (NKJV) and are taken from The Holy Bible: New King James Version (NKJV). Copyright © 1979, 1980, 1982 by Thomas Nelson, Inc. Used by permission. All rights reserved.

Cover Design by Susan Rae Stegall of D/SR Design, LLC
Page Layout by Bart Dawson

ISBN 1-4041-8503-8

Printed in the United States of America

January

1. New Year's Reflections
2. Beginnings
3. Beginnings
4. Changes
5. Winter Warmth
6. Forgiveness
7. Heaven
8. Mothers
9. A Full Quiver
10. Moving
11. Simplification
12. Endings
13. Flexibility
14. Experience
15. Clutter
16. Clutter
17. Hope
18. Winter Warmth
19. Repentance
20. Ties That Bind
21. Homecoming
22. Values
23. Celebration
24. Waging the Battle
25. Obedience
26. Wisdom
27. Wisdom
28. Winter Warmth
29. Waging the Battle
30. Wisdom
31. Sheep

NEW YEAR'S REFLECTIONS

Brethren, I do not count myself to have apprehended; but one thing I do, forgetting those things which are behind and reaching forward to those things which are ahead,

—Philemon 3:13

There is blessing and encouragement in this verse. At this age, most of our deeds are behind us. Among them are much that we would readily forget. Paul here gives us license to do just that. Not only so, but he affirms that there are things that are yet to be done. Let us not retire. Let us strain to grasp the good that lies ahead. By grace, we will acquit ourselves better tomorrow than we did yesterday.

——— DEAR LORD, ———

Help us to put away those things which are passed. Christ's blood covers them so that the Lord will not see them. He has made us new. Let us live like it.

BEGINNINGS

But we are bound to give thanks to God always for you, brethren beloved by the Lord, because God from the beginning chose you for salvation through sanctification by the Spirit and belief in the truth,

—2 Thessalonians 2:13

A t our age, thoughts turn more readily to endings than beginnings. But origins should always be in our minds and hearts. If God loves us, we may be comforted to know that it has been so from before time. Moreover, having fixed His love upon us, He will never let us go. When the world can find no rest, and night brings no peace to the wayward soul, we may sleep the sleep of the loved.

——— FATHER OF ALL COMFORT, ———

The world about us is in tumult. No sleep will come to many on this night. But, the objects of Your grace will rest in the security of knowing that You will see us safely home.

BEGINNINGS

And: "You, Lord, in the beginning laid the foundation of the earth, and the heavens are the work of Your hands."

—Hebrews 1:10

There is much discussion in our day concerning the earth's beginning. The "old time religion" is mocked and driven, along with its God, from the classroom. The theories of unregenerate men multiply and change. Are we to rest our souls upon this shifting sand? The hammers of men's speculations have beat upon the anvil of revealed truth for millennia. When all of the implements of hate and unbelief are broken and cast aside, God's truth will remain.

——— ENDURING LORD, ———

We are thankful that You have begun a good work in us. We cannot truly imagine where it will end, but we know that it will be eternal, and glorious.

CHANGES

...in a moment, in the twinkling of an eye, at the last trumpet. For the trumpet will sound, and the dead will be raised incorruptible, and we shall be changed.

—1 Corinthians 15:52

We are at an age when we are apt to dislike change. The melody has gone from song and has been replaced by meter-less, rhyme-less doggerel. Respect has disappeared from love, and the packer at the super market does not call us sir or ma'am anymore. Still, it is a small comfort to know that I, who am so much in need of alteration, remain much the same. Someday I will be changed. My improvement shall be both total and eternal.

——— UNCHANGEABLE LORD, ———

We grow old in an era of alteration. It is good to know that the object our hope is fixed. We thank You for being our anchor in a stormy sea of change.

WINTER WARMTH

Oh, give thanks to the God of gods! For His mercy endures forever.

—Psalms 136:2

My wife says that I have a bad habit of holding on to old slights. I might suppress them for years, but in the crucible of some stress, they will surface. I am so glad that the Lord is not like that. Should He care to recall just one sin forgiven, I would be destroyed in the heat of His anger. But, His mercy endures forever. I can curl up with that truth on a cold winter's night.

——— MERCIFUL GOD, ———

What great kindness You have bestowed on us. We have long been at enmity with You, but in the midst of our rebellion You extended mercy to us. We thank You for that.

FORGIVENESS

Then Jesus said, "Father, forgive them, for they do not know what they do." And they divided His garments and cast lots.

—Luke 23:34

Let us find hope and confidence here. The Roman government, the religious leaders, and the Jews had, in concert, taken the Lord and with wicked hands crucified Him. Well might these have been especially cursed of God, and estranged from ever finding mercy. But, in fact, they are particularly singled out for clemency. There may we, though fully as vile as these, find forgiveness in the work of Christ. Perhaps in eternity we may together rejoice in the goodness of God.

—— WONDERFUL SAVIOR, ——

How will we ever find the words to praise You as we ought? Give us a vision of the place from which we were rescued. That will tune our voices for thanksgiving.

HEAVEN

For Christ has not entered the holy places made with hands, which are copies of the true, but into heaven itself, now to appear in the presence of God for us;

—Hebrews 9:24

Our hearts are inclined to heaven. The brightness and beauty of it beguile our minds, and draw us upon our journey. But, there is a sense in which we are already in that place. For Christ is there and He is making intercession for us with the Father. We stumble in our pilgrimage, and would be shut out of heaven except Christ pleads for us. His work saves our place so that we may someday find rest there at last.

—— HEAVENLY FATHER, ——

We begin to see the old faces, and the sound of departed voices call to us. Whet our hearts for that land. There we will come to rest in You. It is enough!

MOTHERS

And he who curses his father or his mother shall surely be put to death.

—Exodus 21:17

There is a lot of cursing in our day. There is nothing that remains out of bounds. It seems that the nearer the heart, the greater the curse that is uttered. There is no human relationship that is more sacred than that which is between mother and child. How foul is the mouth that will profane it? The Lord is serious about these things. If you have guilt in this matter, seek forgiveness from Him today.

——— HEAVENLY FATHER, ———

We are a people of unclean lips. Our perversions are without limits. Help us to repent, and to escape the death that results from our curses.

A FULL QUIVER

Like arrows in the hand of a warrior, so are the children of one's youth. Happy is the man who has his quiver full of them; They shall not be ashamed, But shall speak with their enemies in the gate.

—Psalms 127:4, 5

Our children are likened to arrows. Few things are as pleasurable as a house full of kids. As a grandparent, I suppose it may be added that there are few pleasures as sweet as sending them home in the evening. It is the job of parents to direct these little missiles toward a worthy target. Let us aim them in the direction of heaven. What harm can come to those who have an eternal legacy?

—— HEAVENLY FATHER, ——

We thank You that You have given to each of us young people over whom we have influence. Let us use our sway to point them toward heaven and service.

MOVING

"Pass through the camp and command the people, saying, 'Prepare provisions for yourselves, for within three days you will cross over this Jordan, to go in to possess the land which the Lord your God is giving you to possess.'"

—Joshua 1:11

My wife and I used to look at new homes. It was a form of entertainment. I don't recall that we very often looked at places that were less nice that the one we owned. Sometimes I would wonder what it would be like if someone were to give me one of those nice residences. Oh, to be in the shoes of these Israelites. They were about to move into a very nice neighborhood. God was picking up the entire tab.

——— HEAVENLY FATHER, ———

We are like the Israelites of old. We are pilgrims in the land. We have found no place of rest in this desert. Lead us into the Promised Land.

SIMPLIFICATION

Then Peter said, "Silver and gold I do not have, but what I do have I give you: In the name of Jesus Christ of Nazareth, rise up and walk."

—Acts 3:6

I find myself in a "giveaway" mode. Over the years, I have collected too much stuff. Someday I may move to a smaller place, and then I don't know what I will do. It is time to simplify.

Peter seemed to have a good grasp of what was important to have and what must be given away. He did not keep much gold, but he gave away a lot of truth.

——— LORD, ———

Help me to know what is valuable. Give me the sense to garner the good things. Show me the things that only way me down. Help me to get rid of those.

ENDINGS

"Who can count the dust of Jacob, or number one-fourth of Israel? Let me die the death of the righteous, and let my end be like his!"
—Numbers 23:10

The old prophet Balaam had a good grasp of reality. Since all must die, let our end be the end of the righteous. We are despised as the Moabites here despised Israel. Yet, many are the children of grace. We are as the dust: innumerable. Though blessed here, we are destined for even better things. Death for the righteous is only the threshold to a glorious eternity. May it please God to gather us there– and our children also.

RIGHTEOUS FATHER,

We thank You that we may be numbered among the righteous. It is a standing that we do not have in ourselves. It is the righteousness of Christ imputed to us.

FLEXIBILITY

...who will transform our lowly body that it may be conformed to His glorious body, according to the working by which He is able even to subdue all things to Himself.

—Philemon 3:21

I am growing old. I don't like change. My books should always be returned to the same place on the library shelf. My eggs must always be over-medium. But, there are a lot of things about myself that must be revised. These are mostly the result of my condition under sin. Some day, that will all be corrected. Until then, I must flex to effect every alteration that brings me closer to the image of Jesus.

——— WONDERFUL SAVIOR, ———

Your Word tells us that we are both saved and being saved. We must be about the work of sanctification. Help us to become more like You.

EXPERIENCE

A little sleep, a little slumber, a little folding of the hands to rest; So shall your poverty come like a prowler, and your need like an armed man.

—Proverbs 24:33, 34

Experience has taught us that some of the folks in poverty deserve to be there. They spend too much time on the couch, and not enough in pursuit of a living. Similarly, if we would have spiritual riches, we must work for them. We need to be often in the Word, and frequently about the Lord's service. Alternately, we can sit with arms folded. Every life that touches ours will be the poorer for it.

——— JUST LORD, ———

We pray that You will protect us from sloth in all things. Especially, do not let us neglect our duty in the things that pertain to the Kingdom.

Clutter

> "And do not fear those who kill the body but cannot kill the soul. But rather fear Him who is able to destroy both soul and body in hell."
> —Matthew 10:28

On furlough from the navy, my son challenged me saying, "Dad you have lied to me." "How so son," I asked? "You said that the bigger they are the harder they fall." "So?" "The real truth is that the bigger they are the bigger the beating you are about to get!" It is important, in life, to be afraid of the right things. Don't let unwarranted fears clutter your life. Fear God! Everything else is small potatoes.

——— Protector and Friend, ———

What a sense of security Your people have in the face of innumerable forces, any one of which might easily overcome us. You are our protector and our high tower.

CLUTTER

You are not restricted by us, but you are restricted by your own affections.

—2 Corinthians 6:12

The Corinthian church did not love the apostle Paul as they ought. He wanted them to know that his love for them was great. Like these of old, our lives are cluttered with a devotion to that which is unworthy of us. To dote upon things or places is to grasp at the mist—because they pass away. Reserve your affections for that which is of eternal substance. You will have endless ages to love God and His children.

——— LOVING SAVIOR, ———

Only You are worthy. Guide us into proper affections. Keep us from loving riches that pass away. Fix our fondness upon eternal things.

HOPE

*"The Lord is my portion," says my soul,
"Therefore I hope in Him!"*

—Lamentations 3:24

The scripture teaches that nobility, worldly wisdom, and fleshly strength have mostly been doled out to others. We are, as the world would view it, "foolish things." It is no surprise then, that most of us do not have a big slice of the temporal pie. We must expect to obtain our portion in Christ. He is our very great reward. When every worldly thing has passed away, we shall have just begun to enjoy the riches we have in Him.

—— OUR HOPE AND OUR SALVATION, ——

The world expects that larger portions will be meted out to the rich and influential. But, those shall have more of Christ in heaven that were most satisfied with Him here.

WINTER WARMTH

"So it shall be, while My glory passes by, that I will put you in the cleft of the rock, and will cover you with My hand while I pass by."

— Exodus 33:22

Moses desired to see the Lord. But, the sight would have been too much. So the Lord hid him in the cleft of a rock and covered him with His hand while the beauty of His goodness passed in procession. Some day, the anger and justice of God will be displayed. In that day, He will hide me in Jesus, and cover me in His righteousness. I will wrap myself in that truth on this cold winter's evening.

——— BEAUTIFUL SAVIOR, ———

We thank You for the loveliness of Your grace toward us. We would be consumed by Your wrath, except You found a place of safety for us in Jesus Christ.

REPENTANCE

"I tell you, no; but unless you repent you will all likewise perish."

—Luke 13:3

We live in a time when the gospel is distorted. A message of remorse and turning is a hard sell. Better to ease the rules a little. Few things will thin out a church crowd faster than a call for repentance. But, the issue is of the utmost seriousness, so we can't afford to be wrong. If we are in error on this point–we perish. God will not tolerate sin. If we love sin, He will not tolerate us.

——— FORGIVING SAVIOR, ———

Help us to be serious in the matter of repentance. Help us to see that it is an issue of love. We cannot have affection for that which our Lord hates.

TIES THAT BIND

So Sarah died in Kirjath Arba (that is, Hebron) in the land of Canaan, and Abraham came to mourn for Sarah and to weep for her.
— Genesis 23:2

Sarah was Abraham's companion through so much. Now she is dead and her husband comes to weep for her. She was the last link that bound him to Ur: the place of his birth. Sarah has exited this world and is in the arms of the Savior. There are no more tears for her. Abraham mourns, but not as one without hope. He will see her again in that land where comes no more parting.

—— COMFORTING FATHER, ——

Our lives are full of partings. Death tears our dear ones from our side, leaving wounds that do not completely heal in this life. Comfort us with the certainty of heavenly reunion.

HOMECOMING

"See, the day is coming to an end; lodge here, that your heart may be merry. Tomorrow go your way early, so that you may get home."
—Judges 19:9

We are no strangers to the actuarial tables. We know that there are not many two-hundred-year-old people. Things are coming to a close. It would be hard for us to make merry in light of this fact except that we are on our way to other venues. These surroundings are good, but those are better. We can be cheerful as the night approaches because we are eager to get on to a better place.

——— HEAVENLY FATHER, ———

How can we be glad when we know that the end approaches? It is because we move on to a more glorious place. Help us to be merry on our way.

VALUES

He who walks with integrity walks securely, but he who perverts his ways will become known.

— Proverbs 10:9

It has become fashionable to mock the values of our fathers. We delude ourselves that the old fashioned virtue of integrity is obsolete in our day. We accept corruption in the personal lives of our leaders and are surprised that they do not function uprightly. We teach our young that ethics are "situational," and that any wrong may be justified under the right conditions. To paraphrase the old political question: "Are we better off than we were a generation ago?"

——— RIGHTEOUS FATHER, ———

We are corrupt persons in the midst of a foolish and perverse people. Lord, we know that You are just if You send the most severe punishment on us, but if You will—send us mercy.

CELEBRATION

On the third day there was a wedding in Cana of Galilee...

—John 2:1

The old reform catechisms tell us that the whole purpose of our lives is that we should glorify God. Our marital union is not exempt. How blessed are we if we have wedded one who helps us toward that end! Marriage is, in and of itself, a festive event, and the remembrance of it should be a gala occasion also. Let us thank the Lord for Christian spouses. Our every need has been foreseen in His divine ordination.

———— GREAT PROVIDER, ————

You have taught us the importance and holiness of marriage. We thank You that You have provided everything that we need for our pilgrimage.

WAGING THE BATTLE

Put on the whole armor of God, that you may be able to stand against the wiles of the devil.
— Ephesians 6:11

If one is going to an axe fight, it is better for them if they bring an axe. That seems kind of basic, but many of us Christians do not grasp the principle. We have no choice but to engage in spiritual warfare. We can't win this contest by bringing our own wit, tactics and implements. We need weapons from God's arsenal. He gladly supplies all that we need for both an impenetrable defense and an irresistible offense.

— MIGHTY CONQUEROR, —

We would be in fear of the battle except that we know that You have prevailed over all things before us. Give us a renewed assurance that the victory is certain.

OBEDIENCE

"Today you have proclaimed the Lord to be your God, and that you will walk in His ways and keep His statutes, His commandments, and His judgments, and that you will obey His voice."

—Deuteronomy 26:17

We are invited to remember the day that we claimed the Lord Jesus, and also to recall that we proclaimed that relationship to all that would hear. He is Lord. When we get a proper grasp of that truth, it cannot fail to affect our relationship to Him. If we can come to a right understanding of the Lord's opinion, we must recognize that we are not entitled to another. Jesus is Lord. We are content to obey.

—— PATIENT FATHER, ——

There is a great comfort in being under Your command. We are too dull to order ourselves. You direction will not fail, nor lead us into dark places.

WISDOM

"that he may give me the cave of Machpelah which he has, which is at the end of his field. Let him give it to me at the full price, as property for a burial place among you."

—Genesis 23:9

It is a sad day for Abraham. He is seeking a place to bury Sarah, his wife. We would be justified from the context to believe that her death was sudden and unexpected. There is profound wisdom in the one subtle remark: There was a burial place "at the end of his field." We are often asked, "What field are you in?" No matter the answer to that question, remember this—at the end of it is a grave.

——— FATHER IN HEAVEN, ———

Our thoughts never fall upon our death, except that it evokes a fear in our hearts. Lord, we pray that we shall mark a triumphal end, and be comforted in that hour by Your grace.

WISDOM

"In My Father's house are many mansions; if it were not so, I would have told you. I go to prepare a place for you."

—John 14:2

We spend our whole lives with an ambition to upgrade. We come to this age with a bit of wisdom in this regard. We are not creatures of time or of the world. We are made for better things. We have no desire for an earthly mansion of any size, we would care to be in the "Father's House." I know that we will be welcomed there because the Lord Jesus has prepared a place for us.

——— HEAVENLY LORD, ———

We are overwhelmed at the love that You bear for us. We long to be with You in Your Father's house. We know that our place there was purchased at an awful cost.

WINTER WARMTH

For I am persuaded that neither death nor life, nor angels nor principalities nor powers, nor things present nor things to come, nor height nor depth, nor any other created thing, shall be able to separate us from the love of God which is in Christ Jesus our Lord.

—Romans 8:38, 39

We live in a world of separation. We are often parted from our money. Friends don't stick with us as in the past. The love of our children grows cold. Our spouses find another with whom to grow old. Death dissolves the tie that binds. We may be separated from every worldly thing. Doesn't it warm the soul to know that nothing can sever us from the love of God that is in Christ Jesus?

———— CONSTANT REDEEMER, ————

Life has shown us that little which involves the flesh can be relied on. But, You are constant. You have fixed Your love upon us, and You will not let us go.

WAGING THE BATTLE

Therefore take up the whole armor of God, that you may be able to withstand in the evil day, and having done all, to stand.

—Ephesians 6:13

There is a comfort here that may be missed for its subtlety. We have no choice but to fight. The fact that we are light guarantees that we are in opposition to darkness. We have assurance in the spiritual sense that the devil cannot harm us. Here's the truth that will relieve us of some stress: We are only responsible to do all and to stand. We are not responsible to win. Christ Himself will do that.

—— MIGHTY GOD, ——

We are weak creatures. Without Your strength, we cannot triumph over the forces that oppose us. But, we are powerful in Your might. Help us to stand in the day of battle.

WISDOM

"The fear of the Lord is the beginning of wisdom, and the knowledge of the Holy One is understanding."

—Proverbs 9:10

One is on the threshold of wisdom when fear of God awakens in the heart. We churn along our various paths, and are perfectly content to live without acknowledging our Creator. But grace begins to ruffle the exterior of our confidence. By the gospel, we begin to sense the awful consequence of coming before God in Judgment. Fear will lead us to despair. Despair will throw us on Christ. He is the Holy One of God who gives understanding.

——— AWESOME GOD, ———

We thank You that You have given us grace to glimpse Your awful justice. We fear to enter Your presence, except as we are covered in the blood of Christ.

SHEEP

Pride goes before destruction, and a haughty spirit before a fall.

—Proverbs 16:18

There is just nothing more pathetic than a sheep that will not admit that he or she is a sheep. Backward and stupid, they prefer that they are something a little higher up the food chain. There is no hope for a sheep until it comes to a place where it will admit its "sheephood." Sadly, some never come to this truth. These continue to wander until they fall into something. Oftentimes, it is the grave.

——— BLESSED CREATOR, ———

Remove from me my foolish pride. Help me to acknowledge my needy condition. Let me find in You that which I must have to make me whole.

February

1. Gleaning
2. Servanthood
3. Winter Warmth
4. Triumph
5. Passing it On
6. Glory
7. A Full Quiver
8. Fellowship
9. Grief
10. Obedience
11. Beginnings
12. Repentance
13. Changes
14. Crowns
15. Giving
16. Winter Warmth
17. Holiness
18. Wisdom
19. Hope
20. Passing It On
21. Ties That Bind
22. Wisdom
23. Wisdom
24. Brothers and Sisters
25. Sheep
26. Triumph
27. Ties That Bind
28. Winter Warmth

GLEANING

Thus says the Lord of hosts: "They shall thoroughly glean as a vine the remnant of Israel; as a grape-gatherer, put your hand back into the branches."

—Jeremiah 6:9

Jeremiah cried out in warning. Destruction hung ominously above a wayward and rebellious people. The enemy would strip the land, gathering all the nourishment, even that which would feed the most determined gleaner. If God did not spare the Israel of old, will He excuse us? Don't presume on the goodness of God! The fruit of the gospel hangs low today, and you may pick of it freely. Evil days may come when no man can harvest truth.

——— BOUNTIFUL SAVIOR, ———

We thank You that You put Your gospel within the reach of every man. We pray that it will always be so. Do not hide Your face from us, lest we die.

SERVANTHOOD

So he built an altar there and called on the name of the Lord, and he pitched his tent there; and there Isaac's servants dug a well.

—Genesis 26:25

Here are servants at work. They do not give direction. They receive that from the master. The do not make the plan, but are content to execute the plan of another. May we be employed like these humble men. They dig a well so that those who follow them may drink deeply and live. We, by grace, may do the same. Let us rise early, work long, and sleep well knowing that we have been about the Master's business.

MASTER,

We have no better use than to be about the work of Your Kingdom. Let each of us humbly walk in the path of service until You come.

WINTER WARMTH

What then shall we say to these things? If God is for us, who can be against us?

—Romans 8:31

During the course of my sojourn, there have been those that opposed me. Doubtless, some had good reason. Others simply did not like me. Satan hates me. He has not the capacity to love me. Much of what he might allege contains the truth. How good it is on this winter's day to know that God is for me. If that is so, then what cares have I? When I let myself consider this, I simply do not know what to say!

——— MERCIFUL MASTER, ———

There can be no doubt that we have sinned, and Your justice is sure to find it out. How can we ever thank You that You put our punishment upon the Lord Jesus Christ?

TRIUMPH

"Look!" he answered, "I see four men loose, walking in the midst of the fire; and they are not hurt, and the form of the fourth is like the Son of God."

—Daniel 3:25

Three Jewish lads have been thrown into a furnace because they would not bow themselves to idols. The oven is incredibly hot, but the men are not consumed. In fact, they walk about as though the flame had no power at all over them. The world may do as it will with us. Still, they have no ultimate power over God's children. He is with us in the fire. He will deliver us. Christ is our victory!

PROTECTOR AND DEFENDER,

We are weak and no match for the enemies that surround us. If You do not protect us, we are lost. Your faithfulness is our security, and our defense from our adversary.

PASSING IT ON

"Moses My servant is dead. Now therefore, arise, go over this Jordan, you and all this people, to the land which I am giving to them-- the children of Israel."

—Joshua 1:2

Israel had only known one leader. Now Moses is dead. He was a handsome man, polished in the courts of the world's greatest power. By his hand; Egypt is a memory ruined and humbled. The loss of Moses is no small thing. However, God is never dependent on any person—no matter how great or gifted. The work of the Lord will continue. Put an end to your grieving, and get on your feet! There is much to do!

——— TRIUMPHANT LORD, ———

We thank You that our hope does not depend on any earthly person. These fall away, but You remain. Help us to see the security that lies in this truth.

GLORY

Now Joshua said to Achan, "My son, I beg you, give glory to the Lord God of Israel, and make confession to Him, and tell me now what you have done; do not hide it from me."

—Joshua 7:19

Achan is in hot water. He has been singled out before all Israel as the culprit. He will die shortly because He has disobeyed God. This final fleeting opportunity is offered to him to glorify God in confession. Glorifying God is so important that should we have only minutes to live, our time would be best spent in this activity. While we have time and liberty, let us not be slack in according honor to God.

——— GLORIOUS GOD, ———

Help us to see that the days are short in which to glorify You in this life. Let us make this a priority because of Your worthiness, as our end approaches.

A FULL QUIVER

After he begot Seth, the days of Adam were eight hundred years; and he had sons and daughters.

—Genesis 5:4

One wonders if Eve dressed the little girls in pink and the boys in blue. How good is God that He should so bless Adam in spite of all his faults! A remnant of the sons and daughters of this first union have born the torch of faith through trial and tribulation, and are entrusting it now into our hands. Similarly, our children, and theirs, may bear the Truth to future generations as long as the earth stands.

——— FAITHFUL GOD, ———

We bless Your name that You have sent the gospel to us. Let us now be faithful to plant the truth within our children, that they may proclaim it to unborn generations.

FELLOWSHIP

"Take heed to yourselves. If your brother sins against you, rebuke him; and if he repents, forgive him."

—Luke 17:3

I never liked admonitions as a child, and none of my children ever told me that they enjoyed a good reprimand. Looking back, I can see that the motive behind my correction was always love. How can we truly care for another, and see them tend toward harm? This ought to be a part of our Christian fellowship. How often has the wayward puppy found his way back to the paper by means of a loving reproof?

——— HEAVENLY FATHER, ———

We abhor the path that leads away from You. Keep us on the path of obedience. When we stray, do as seems best to You to bring us into fellowship again.

GRIEF

But Esau ran to meet him, and embraced him, and fell on his neck and kissed him, and they wept.

—Genesis 33:4

At one time, Esau had desired to kill his brother. A good case could be made that Jacob deserved his brother's wrath. Whatever the respective merits or blame, the brothers have been separated a long while and now meet again. They grieve for what is lost. Esau's anger, and Jacob's deception have taken from each that which neither can replace. Since Christ has forgiven us much, let us for His sake be reconciled to one another.

——— FORGIVING SAVIOR, ———

Help us to forgive each other. Let us not carry the burden of hate or revenge. Help us to be like You, who have forgiven us so much.

OBEDIENCE

If they obey and serve Him, they shall spend their days in prosperity, and their years in pleasures.

—Job 36:11

"Don't go there," I warned my toddler son. I could see a decision process at work in his little mind. Suddenly, he made a move in the forbidden direction. Had I not loved him, I might have been deflected by the surface cuteness. But, love will always correct. He won an exchange that traded his temporary comfort for future prosperity and pleasure. To allow those we love to go on without rebuke is to stoke the fires of their ruin.

DEAR LORD,

Bring us by Your grace into a perfect obedience. Outside of Your will are all of the pains of rebellion. Inside are all the joys of Your care.

BEGINNINGS

...without father, without mother, without genealogy, having neither beginning of days nor end of life, but made like the Son of God, remains a priest continually.

—Hebrews 7:3

Our Scriptures are not an explanation. They are a revelation. What we are told in this verse boggles our minds: Christ had no beginning of days. There is more than a puzzlement here—there is a blessing also! This One who had no beginning has no ending either. That is good news! As long as He shall live, we shall live also. Because He lives, our eyes will see the glory of an unending succession of eternal mornings.

——— ETERNAL FATHER, ———

Our minds cannot grasp eternity. It is a good thing, for the glory of it might slay us. By grace we have begun along this endless road. Our hearts well up in thanks.

REPENTANCE

"And now, here we are, in your hands; do with us as it seems good and right to do to us."
—Joshua 9:25

The Gibeonites were a tribe living in the path of God's vengeance. Victorious Israelite armies were under orders to slay every individual in Canaan. Through a deception, these people gained a promise of exemption. Now they have been caught in their lies. Their demeanor is such as might be emulated by every repentant soul: "I have done wrong. You would be just to slay me." God will honor a broken heart. He will forgive us for Christ's sake.

——— FORGIVING SAVIOR, ———

Break our hearts over this matter of sin. Show us the great grace of forgiveness. You would be fair to slay us. Your mercy is great toward us.

CHANGES

And such were some of you. But you were
washed, but you were sanctified, but you were
justified in the name of the Lord Jesus and by
the Spirit of our God.

—1 Corinthians 6:11

It is good, on rare occasions, to recall what
we were before grace found us. We sat in
dark places, and were content to do so. The
rank feculence of sin clung to us. The chasm
of the pit yawned before us. We maintained
an active hatred for God, and saw nothing in
righteousness to be desired. He has saved us
from that. Jesus washed us and made us clean.
We are changed and there is no going back!

——— CHANGELESS FATHER, ———

We acknowledge that we are a fainting and
fickle people. We bless You for Your patience,
and correction. You are a certain refuge from
all that besets us.

CROWNS

And everyone who competes for the prize is temperate in all things. Now they do it to obtain a perishable crown, but we for an imperishable crown.

—1 Corinthians 9:25

Everything about us is perishable. Oftentimes, that is a good thing. Those fashions that had such appeal then, seem rather horrid today. It is sobering to look around and appraise the things that I have striven to obtain. Perishable! All perishable! I pray God that all that I have earned, by His grace, shall not be paid out to me in coin of this realm. May I win that crown, which shall never fade, nor decay.

——— OUR GREAT REWARD, ———

These truths are too deep for us. You first ordained our good works, then You gave us grace to do them. Truly we must lay our crowns at Your feet. All else would be unjust.

GIVING

It is good to give thanks to the Lord, and to sing praises to Your name, O Most High;

—Psalms 92:1

In any consideration of giving, we must treat the matter of thanksgiving. We are so disposed to plead earnestly with God for some gift. Upon receiving, we are prone to simply go on to the next petition. This does not please God, and it is not good for us. We need to understand that God is the source of all gifts. Our hearts shall not pulse again unless by His leave. Pause now and give thanks for all God has given you.

——— GIVING FATHER, ———

You have laded our lives with every good thing. We are apt to vaunt ourselves and entertain the thought that we are deserving. Keep us from such stupid pride.

WINTER WARMTH

My flesh and my heart fail; but God is the strength of my heart and my portion forever.

—Psalms 73:26

Cold weather is a good time to test your physical systems. If you are still of a mind to shovel your drive, that is an excellent cardiac test. Of course, if you fail the exam there you are on your face in the drive. Better to curl up by the fire with something warm. Try this: Think about having a portion of an infinite God. No one can tax Him. He won't wear out. Neither will we, by His grace.

—— EVERLASTING FATHER, ——

Each day brings a new reminder of our mortality. How good it is to see You more clearly each day as the world, and our attachment to it, fades.

HOLINESS

For God did not call us to uncleanness, but in holiness.

—1 Thessalonians 4:7

We are by nature unclean beings. We desire the smutty and the false. Additionally, we don't want to be around anyone who would remind us that this is so. We won't listen to a politician who would reform us, or a preacher who would condemn us. Our situation is pretty desperate. We won't be changed, and God won't have us the way we are! Unless grace should apprehend us and change us, we are lost.

——— HOLY FATHER, ———

We are so wedded to our filth. We could have no part in You unless You would clean us and make us pure. Thank You for the grace of holiness.

WISDOM

Now it came to pass after these things that God tested Abraham, and said to him, "Abraham!" And he said, "Here I am."

—Genesis 22:1

My wise old father told me, "Son there's always something." Since then, I have noticed that when I come to the top of a long hill, and I might expect a nice downhill coast, the runner will come off my sled. Abraham expected this summons would bring good news, but before the interview was over, Abraham was commanded to sacrifice his son. Wisdom is in knowing that our trials are meant to mature and bless us.

——— LOVING TEACHER, ———

We know that when we have an eternity to ponder, we shall see that some of our greatest blessings came to us wrapped in trial. We thank You for the eternal lessons learned.

HOPE

When a wicked man dies, his expectation will perish, and the hope of the unjust perishes.

—Proverbs 11:7

The stock market has crashed, but we hope for a rise tomorrow. The doctor's diagnosis is one from which few recover, but perhaps we will beat the odds. There is that within us that will not be denied some prospect of betterment. Our scripture tells us that there is a point at which hope perishes. The sinner who falls into the hands of an angry God, can and does expect nothing. Thank God we have made our peace with Him.

—— OUR HOPE AND OUR SALVATION, ——

Let this be a spur to our witness. There are those all about us who approach the pit. Help us to warn them, and point them toward the Savior.

PASSING IT ON

Till I come, give attention to reading, to exhortation, to doctrine.

—1 Timothy 4:13

We are to pass it on, but it is not just anything that we please. We must give the scripture a central place (reading). We are not commanded to sing it, mime it, or dramatize it—we are called to preach it (exhort). Pius platitudes won't do—it is doctrine that we must tell. There is a sense of urgency here, and it gladdens my heart. The Lord is coming again. A day approaches when faith will be supplanted by sight.

——— TRIUMPHANT LORD, ———

Away with all that itching ears desire. Help us to pass on truth. It is an offense to the world, but it is the truth of God.

TIES THAT BIND

God is faithful, by whom you were called into the fellowship of His Son, Jesus Christ our Lord.

—1 Corinthians 1:9

When we are all assembled we are remarkable for our dissimilarity. Our colors are as varied as the rainbow. Our languages are many as the nations. Some of us can read, and others remain illiterate. Our time is from the creation, and we will remain until the end. While nothing else binds us together, we all warm to the name of the Lord. Jesus has bought us and wrapped us in a fellowship of love.

——— AUTHOR OF LOVE, ———

We thank You that You have made us one. Help us to love one another. For since we, who are so unlovely, have been received by Your love, how shall we not love another?

WISDOM

Jesus said to him, "I am ...the truth ..."

—John 14:6

What is truth? That was an easier question in our youth. Sadly, the modern world is pretty much opposed to anything learned at our mother's knee. We live in an era of "spin." We accept that a portion of every message contains some untruth.

How comforting to know that Jesus is still the truth! We may trust our eternal souls to Him. Years and men vanish into nothingness, but His Word will never pass away.

——— ALL-WISE FATHER, ———

You have saved us from the foolishness of this world and from the lies of the devil. We ourselves will see the fiery destruction of present things, but Your truth will remain.

WISDOM

Now to him who works, the wages are not counted as grace but as debt.

—Romans 4:4

One cannot be counted as wise at our age if they do not know the value of things on the market. A reasoned assessment of our value in terms of wages would be included in those estimations. Our problem arises in the spiritual realm. There we are reckoned to be dead! Such does not bring much on the Soul Exchange. Our best and most sincere efforts would not purchase peace with God. Our only hope lay in the grace of God!

——— WONDERFUL SAVIOR, ———

Keep us from the delusion that we have obtained mercy on our merit. Help us to see that a just wage for our effort is death. Let us glory in Your wonderful grace.

BROTHERS AND SISTERS

Then the Lord said to Cain, "Where is Abel your brother?" He said, "I do not know. Am I my brother's keeper?"

—Genesis 4:9

Cain never found his brother, nor did he ever really find peace. This is due to the fact that he did not "keep" him. There is no greater love between brothers or sisters than that which motivates us to "keep" them. Let us endure difference, rebuke error, tend illness, celebrate victory, keep confidences, share the good, and comfort the sorrows. What will we not do for family, since our brother Jesus has done so much for us?

————— CARING FATHER, —————

We thank You that the family of God is rich in heavenly graces. Help us to extend the goodness that has been shown to us freely upon others.

SHEEP

"...who may go out before them and go in before them, who may lead them out and bring them in, that the congregation of the Lord may not be like sheep which have no shepherd."

—Numbers 27:17

If we were better and smarter and more like our creator, we would not have to be led everywhere. The ugly truth is that there is no point in finding a sheep, and then merely pointing it toward home. The next moment will find it lost again. We must be led all the way into the fold. If we can get by the humbling aspects of this, we will find a great comfort in it.

——— GOOD SHEPHERD, ———

How glad we are that You do not merely set a good example for us. Though we ought to follow You, we are weak and prone to wander. You will lead us all the way home.

TRIUMPH

Now thanks be to God who always leads us in triumph in Christ, and through us diffuses the fragrance of His knowledge in every place.

—2 Corinthians 2:14

My experience in life is that I win some and I lose others. Often, it seems that the loss column is swelling. This could cause the late-night sweats. However, when I take a proper perspective, I realize that the score in non-spiritual matters doesn't matter very much. What I must do daily is follow Christ. Let me spread the sweet savor of His love and forgiveness. At the end of that road is a dazzling triumph.

——— O GOD, OUR TRIUMPH, ———

Help us to follow You in humble obedience. Let us be a blessing to those whose lives we touch. Cause us to see that victory not in ourselves, but in our God.

TIES THAT BIND

"You shall love the Lord your God with all your heart, with all your soul, and with all your strength."

—Deuteronomy 6:5

We are bound to the Lord with bonds of affection. It is no wonder that we, His children, should be devoted to Him. He sought us through the black night, and plucked us from perilous places. He bound up our wounds and made us whole and free. If we adore Him, it is because He first cared for us. He wooed our errant and antagonistic hearts by His grace, and caused us to return His Love.

—— ADORED SAVIOR, ——

We thank You for a love that will not let us go. We are weak and wayward and would stray from Your arms, except that You hold us securely for all eternity.

WINTER WARMTH

So then, after the Lord had spoken to them, He was received up into heaven, and sat down at the right hand of God.

—Mark 16:19

My interest in this verse is keen. The truth of it calms my fears, and imbues my soul with warmth. My sin was on Christ as they drove the nails into His hands. They brought death to Him, and caused Him to be laid in a tomb. Now, He has been received by the Father into heaven, and sits by His right hand. What of my sin? Where is it? I cannot answer, but this I know: It is gone!

——— WONDERFUL SAVIOR, ———

I wonder where my sin has gone, but it contents me well to know that it has disappeared. The ages will roll, but it can never find me again. Nor will I ever seek it.

March

IMAGES

"...and build an altar to the Lord your God on top of this rock in the proper arrangement, and take the second bull and offer a burnt sacrifice with the wood of the image which you shall cut down."

—Judges 6:26

If we would live at peace in the Kingdom of God we must do as Gideon is here commanded. We delude ourselves that we can have both God and these little competitors for our love. We should give them no quarter. They must be cut to the ground. Not only so, but they must be burned. Where they have been polluting your service, and signifying your disobedience, the sweet fruits of the Spirit will grow.

——— IMMUTABLE FATHER, ———

It is an outrage that we would honor any other in competition with You. We praise You for withholding Your justice so that we might be the objects of Your mercy.

BROTHERS AND SISTERS

Jesus said to her, "Your brother will rise again."

—John 11:23

Having achieved some age, we have all stood numb with grief, and ravaged by loss before the open grave. At these times, we have drawn the living close and mourned the dead. These words have softened the hardness of the hour. Funerals without Christ are also without hope. This promise, so precious to the family of God, is without comfort to the lost. Brothers and sisters, we will greet one another anew on the resurrection morning!

———— RESURRECTED SAVIOR, ————

We would mourn our dead, but not too deeply, or too overly long. This would dishonor You who have made us Heirs to such rich promises that we shall meet again.

RETIREMENT

You have not yet resisted to bloodshed, striving against sin.

—Hebrews 12:4

There is a malady that sweeps over people who reach a "certain age." They have this lemming-like urge to withdraw from life and flee to the sidelines. Let the youth fight the battles. Let them know the blood of combat as we have experienced it. The writer here disallows such an attitude. We are not exempted from the fray. We must press the battle until the last breath. We cannot give up. We're not dead yet.

———— FATHER OF OUR REST, ————

We know that we shall come at last into Your rest. Show us that the time for ease is not yet. Imbue us with a renewed energy for Your work.

GLEANING

"And you shall not glean your vineyard, nor shall you gather every grape of your vineyard; you shall leave them for the poor and the stranger: I am the Lord your God."
—Leviticus 19:10

We were once strangers to the grace of God. Our spirits were parched and dry, for we were poor in spiritual things. The long days passed and there was naught to nourish our souls. One glorious day, a drop of grace fell from the lips of a preacher, or a friend, and we did hasten to take it in. Since then, it has been a well within us, springing up into life eternal. We shall never hunger or thirst again.

—— WONDERFUL PROVIDER, ——
We were strangers to grace, and steeped in spiritual poverty. Since You sought us and made us children, we have dined daily from the lavish table of Your grace.

RELATIONSHIPS

"No longer do I call you servants, for a servant does not know what his master is doing; but I have called you friends, for all things that I heard from My Father I have made known to you."

—John 15:15

One thing that persons of our age should have learned is exactly how they relate in the grand scheme of things. Nothing can be more important, in this regard, than how we relate to Christ. He spoke everything into existence. They continue by His sufferance. It is Christ that will ultimately judge all things. Consider His greatness and our obscurity. What condescension that He should permit us, who have placed our faith in Him, to call Him "friend."

——— DEAR FATHER, ———

There is no relationship in our lives that is not brightened by our kinship to You. Help us to be a blessing to others, by helping them to know You.

GIVING

"For God so loved the world that He gave His only begotten Son, that whoever believes in Him should not perish but have everlasting life."

—John 3:16

Any consideration of giving must begin here. Love will always find a way to give. A great love is betokened by a momentous sacrifice. The gift here spoken of is lavish indeed. This was not just God's Son, but His only Son. A ransom of infinite value is paid to redeem that which, absent love, is worthless. Eternal life is free to the recipient. All attempts at purchases are rebuffed. Only empty hands may grasp everlasting life!

——— GIVER OF LIFE, ———

What can we say? It is grace that caused our soul to quake. Grace opened our eyes to our peril. It led us to Christ who proffered forgiveness. It was Your wonderful gift.

SPRINGTIME REFLECTIONS

I remember the days of old; I meditate on all Your works; I muse on the work of Your hands.

—Psalms 143:5

What better time to muse on the works of God's hands than in springtime? Yesterday the earth was hard with frost, but today tender shoots appear. God is bringing life out of death. He has done the same with us. Our hearts were hard from long winters of unbelief. He softened our hearts and made them beat again. Once we could not see God. Now we see Him in the birth and beauty of Spring.

— MIGHTY GOD, —

Our minds cannot begin to comprehend the things that You have done. The universe knows no bounds. Every day we see new and beautiful wonders from Your hands.

IGNORANCE

But if anyone is ignorant, let him be
ignorant.

—1 Corinthians 14:38

I sat at a table during the wedding reception
of a friend's daughter. Perhaps it was I that
set the tone, but all of the remaining chairs
were soon filled with old men. I turned the
conversation to biblical truth. I was greatly
disappointed in the ignorance that was
displayed there. I returned home thanking
God that He had not allowed me to reach their
age immersed in such ignorance. Let us work so
that others should not do so either.

——— OMNISCIENT FATHER, ———

Cause us to know more of You. We are finite,
and You are infinite, so we will never learn all.
Show Yourself to us so that we can love You
more.

SHEEP

"For I know this, that after my departure savage wolves will come in among you, not sparing the flock."

—Acts 20:29

Wolves are everything that sheep are not. They are smart and given to craftiness. They are prettier than sheep. Make them angry and their teeth show. Sheep do not bite–they are bitten. Sheep are no match for wolves. Only a Shepherd who loves them and is willing to face peril for them can protect them against this predator. The Lord has left good men to watch over me. Under His guidance, they will protect me from error and hurt.

 LORD,

Thank You for providing those who direct us to safety. We are grateful for those who will go out into the dark and far places to minister to our souls.

CROWNS

When they had twisted a crown of thorns,
they put it on His head, and a reed in His
right hand. And they bowed the knee before
Him and mocked Him, saying, "Hail, King
of the Jews!"

—Matthew 27:29

The person whose idea this was no doubt congratulated himself for his wit. "We will make a crown of thorns and press it down upon His noble brow. That will draw blood, and the derision of the crowd." It was sin that caused thorns to intrude upon the garden, and it is the same that crafts this cruel crown. The blood flows down regal and red. Blessed is that one who can say at heart, "It was for me."

——— BLESSED SACRIFICE, ———
We cannot think of Your suffering except that it causes within us the greatest thanksgiving. The crown of thorns is the only diadem that we ever justly merited.

MOVING

...therefore the Lord God sent him out of the garden of Eden to till the ground from which he was taken.

—Genesis 3:23

Sin is inconsistent with blessing, and our poor father Adam finds that out. He is booted from the garden. Not only that, but his life of joy and service were exchanged for a life of sweat and labor. It was a huge moving day for him, and us! Lest we learn to dislike Adam overmuch for the grief that he brought upon us, remember that Christ, on this same principle, brings peace and blessing to all that are in Him.

—— HEAVENLY FATHER, ——

We thank You for our father Adam. We thank You for our salvation that brings to us a greater blessing than could have ever been ours from Adam's hand.

EXPERIENCE

"Therefore know that the Lord your God, He is God, the faithful God who keeps covenant and mercy for a thousand generations with those who love Him and keep His commandments;"

—Deuteronomy 7:9

There was a day when a handshake and a pledge could be relied upon. Lawyers in that day were few, as was the need for them. Of what worth is our long walk with God if it has not taught us that His Word is true? Though we are fickle, and change with the wind, He has been trustworthy. On the promise of God, we are content to hang the felicity of our eternal souls.

——— FAITHFUL MASTER, ———
Teach us to trust You. In this world, we cannot be sure of anyone's fidelity. But You are trustworthy. Show us that we are totally and safely dependent on You.

FLEXIBILITY

Now the Lord had said to Abram: "Get out of your country, from your family and from your father's house, to a land that I will show you.

—Genesis 12:1

The scripture tells us that Abram immediately pulled up stakes and left Ur. He was then already seventy-five years old. If he were much like me, he might not have had sufficient flexibility to upset his schemes, and life. That is a real danger for everyone of our age. We must leave room in our plans for the call of God. It just might be, that by the grace of God, our best days are before us.

——— LOVING FATHER, ———

We thank You for the good, and thank You for the years that You have meted out to us. Give us work while the sun yet shines upon us, so that we may be a blessing to others.

FAITH

For by grace you have been saved through faith, and that not of yourselves; it is the gift of God, not of works, lest anyone should boast.

—Ephesians 2:8, 9

It is a comfort to know that faith does not originate in us. There is comfort in knowing that it is a grace from God. I was years in my walk before I realized that. However, there are rich blessings in this truth. Of myself, I am weak, and as unstable as water. What a joy to know that the One who gave me the faith to believe will lead me by His grace until I am safe at home.

——— FATHER OF ALL FAITH, ———

We are puffed up with a sense of our own power. Help us to see our weakness, and bring us to a sense of Your sufficiency.

CROWNS

For what is our hope, or joy, or crown of rejoicing? Is it not even you in the presence of our Lord Jesus Christ at His coming? For you are our glory and joy.

—1 Thessalonians 2:19, 20

By the grace of God, I have been to many interesting places in the world. Some of my journeys have been taken alone. Solitude diminished my joy. I pray that when I get to heaven that I shall not be there by myself. I want to be surrounded by those who have received grace through my servanthood. I want to see those who have lit a torch of truth from my hand. I pray that they will be a multitude!

——— GRACIOUS GOD, ———

Like our brother Paul, we did little think that someday our delight would be in pointing others to Your mercy. We were far from You, but are now made near by Your grace.

A FULL QUIVER

Now the word of the Lord came to Jonah the
son of Amittai...

—Jonah 1:1

It is the way of the Scriptures that they will give us a little genealogy when there is glory or shame to be meted out. Jonah brought glory to God by bearing a message of mercy to Nineveh. It is a joy to note that his father is accorded some honor here by virtue of his parenthood. May a similar recognition be ours as our children distinguish themselves in and by the grace of God!

——— FATHER, ———

Give us grace to minister truth to our children. May it be that they will do the same for their children. Let such honor as comes from this be wholly Yours.

HARD WORK

But Jesus answered them, "My Father has been working until now, and I have been working."

—John 5:17

We know that labor is noble and good because God works. The Lord Jesus rose early to be about His fathers business. He went places that were unpleasant. He did tasks that were beneath him. For our sakes, He faced evil and malignant people. He preached and taught to the point of exhaustion. Great drops of blood came—so earnestly did He intercede for us. What excuse will we offer Him at the judgment for our laziness?

——— DILIGENT SAVIOR, ———

We have worked hard in our lives, and often the reward was scant. Show us our great reward for service in the Kingdom. It will keep us from sloth and idleness.

FLEXIBILITY

'And I will say to my soul, "Soul, you have many goods laid up for many years; take your ease; eat, drink, and be merry."'
—Luke 12:19

Riches are deceptive. They speak a false security to the soul. When we were young and unsettled, we needed to be flexible in order to meet the demands of children, careers, and financial emergencies. If God has blessed us so that we are settled and secure, we need to use care that the sighs of ease do not drown out the call of God. Let us take care that we tend the needs of our souls.

——— GOOD AND GRACIOUS GOD, ———
We have lived these long years from Your kind hand. Let us not presume upon Your goodness. Let us not turn from gratefulness into the path of ease and sloth.

WISDOM

Though He slay me, yet will I trust Him.
—Job 13:15

Oftentimes on our journey, we have come to some very dark and difficult places. The winds of Providence blew heavily on us so that we could scarcely stand. We could see no reason, nor any good that could come from our circumstance. We did not know what He was doing, but we have learned to know Him. Wisdom lies in our trusting God. If we rely on Him to do right, we shall never be ashamed.

——— TRUSTWORTHY LORD, ———
We thank You that You work every event for our good. We may not see Your purpose in this world, but we have an eternity to see its perfection.

SERVANTHOOD

And when Pharaoh saw that the rain, the hail, and the thunder had ceased, he sinned yet more; and he hardened his heart, he and his servants.

—Exodus 9:34

Moses was a servant of the Lord. The servants mentioned in this passage are those of Pharaoh. This is one of many verses that might be used to illustrate that there are no free agents in the war for the Kingdom. Everybody serves somebody! That's a sobering thought, and ought to cause some self-examination. If you tire of the plagues that the Lord sends down on His enemies, pray that God will allow you to switch sides.

——— LORD, ———

We remember our old master. He abused us, and he had no capacity to love us. We are thankful that our new Master did not leave us to perish, but drew us into a lifetime of blessed service.

IMAGES

So God created man in His own image; in the image of God He created him; male and female He created them.

—Genesis 1:27

God, being a Spirit, has no body. How then are men made in His image? Man has an immortal soul. He is never ending. Man has dominion over all else in creation—an authority given by God. He was made in moral purity, that he might know God and fellowship with Him. Man was not created to be God, but to have the impress of God upon him. Only Christ is the express image of the Father.

——— IMMUTABLE FATHER, ———

Our race is wont to make images with our own hands and worship them. We thank You that You have given us a glimpse of Your person, which cannot be reduced to an image.

HARD WORK

"I must work the works of Him who sent Me while it is day; the night is coming when no one can work."

—John 9:4

I have always been a "deadliner." It is a trait that I do not recommend to the reader. I did not study for the exam until the night before the test. It was my wont to rip my presentation off the copier on my way to the meeting. It is sobering, then, to confront this truth. I had better finish my work, and it had better be in good order for I must stand and give account of it to God.

——— RIGHTEOUS JUDGE, ———

Keep us from sloth and indifference. Help us to see Your awful justice so that we do not slack or faint. From whom much is given, much is required.

ENDINGS

And now abide faith, hope, love, these three; but the greatest of these is love.

—1 Corinthians 13:13

These many years, we have clung to Christ by faith. This has produced in us a steadfast hope. How odd to realize that these moorings of our worldly pilgrimage are destined to disappear. In one wondrous and bright instant they will fall away. Then we shall see for ourselves the truth that these old friends betoken. Both shall be dissolved in sight. We will see the One upon whom our soul has trusted. All that need remain is love.

——— LOVING LORD, ———

Though faith and hope are dear to us in this world, we are eager to exchange them at the first sight of You. Until then, we thank You for the comfort that they bring to our lives.

GLORY

For I consider that the sufferings of this present time are not worthy to be compared with the glory which shall be revealed in us.

—Romans 8:18

There is a blessed and intriguing truth here. Our verse discloses a particular aspect of His glory that will be shown in us. One can almost see the heavenly crowd gathering to behold the perfection that we will have become in Christ. We will be first to acknowledge the beauty, but we must confess that the Savior did not have much to work with. We will exclaim, "Grace found us in ruin–but, oh, just look at us now!"

——— TRANSFORMING LORD, ———

We thank You that we are not as You found us. But, we are also not what we shall be. You will make us into examples of Your grace. In this way, we will ever glorify You.

CROWNS

"Be faithful until death, and I will give you the crown of life."

—Revelation 2:10

There was nothing in the red earth of middle Tennessee to prepare my mind for thoughts of crowns. We were humble people in the midst of the same. The rusty tin roof of our four-room house did not speak of royalty. How good then, to think that I shall someday be crowned with life. Not a life such as I have known, nor one such as I deserve. It will be glorious, and it will be eternal!

—— SAVIOR AND KING, ——

Our minds reel that we should ever enter into a discussion of crowns. How rich and good is Your grace that we, an impoverished, and hopeless people should know this joy.

SPRINGTIME REFLECTIONS

It happened in the spring of the year, at the time when kings go out to battle, that David sent Joab and his servants with him, and all Israel; and they destroyed the people of Ammon and besieged Rabbah. But David remained at Jerusalem.

—2 Samuel 11:1

Springtime was a season of activity around our house when I was a child. Mom would take down the lace curtains and secure them to stretchers, which would help them hold their shape. Dad would drain the alcohol from the family auto radiator. The dog would eye us all warily knowing that he had a bath coming.

David did not do his duty as he ought to have done. That failure would make a mountain of trouble for him and the kingdom.

——— LORD, ———

We thank You that we have duties to look after in Your service. Help us to know them, and to take them seriously. Keep us diligent so that no harm can result from our neglect.

PARTING

"But I say to you, I will not drink of this fruit of the vine from now on until that day when I drink it new with you in My Father's kingdom."

—Matthew 26:29

Parting often involves a promise of reunion. Here our Lord readies Himself, and His disciples for a time of severing. He will be torn from them. They will witness the most awful cruelty. How precious then is the attendant promise. They will meet again. All will raise again the glass in celebration of a work perfectly done. In His heaven, no parting tears will be shed. We shall be with Him—at home in the Kingdom.

 KINDLY LORD,

It is a comfort to know that You are no stranger to our grief. Parting has touched Your heart as it has ours. Help us to see a time of reunion. That will quiet our sorrows.

HOPE

Behold, the eye of the Lord is on those who fear Him, on those who hope in His mercy.

—Psalms 33:18

God fixes those who have fled to Him for mercy with a loving eye. He works all things for their good. The times may appear dark about them, but God's protection surrounds them. Their hope for mercy will never be ashamed. They may be weak. Doubts sometimes cloud their joy, but God is faithful in His love for them. He will order their ways aright, and He will not forget His love for them.

—— OUR HOPE AND OUR SALVATION, ——
Often might our foot have slipped and we be dashed upon the rocks. You are our keeper and protector. All of our hope is in You.

BEGINNINGS

For the time has come for judgment to begin at the house of God; and if it begins with us first, what will be the end of those who do not obey the gospel of God?

—1 Peter 4:17

What a sad spectacle is the unexamined life! It is the more pitiable when observed in those who have lived long. Let us turn the eye of Scripture upon ourselves and find those things that are not honoring to God. What does it matter that we should leave a mountain of earthly wealth to heirs, and neglect our spiritual legacy? Yesterday would have been preferred, but what better time remains to us than now?

———— RIGHTEOUS GOD, ————

We thank You for Your forbearance toward us. We repent our past lethargy, and beg for a renewal of Your holiness within, that we might be useful servants for Your Kingdom.

CELEBRATION

Now Elizabeth's full time came for her to be
delivered, and she brought forth a son.
—Luke 1:57

Few things fill the heart with as much joy
as the birth of a child. Picking a name,
readying a room, selecting infant's clothes,
anticipating genius, expecting good looks, and
inclining innocent little ones in the direction
of God's grace are all elements of this supreme
joy. Have we celebrated our children today?
Have we thanked the One who has given us
every good and perfect gift? Oh, that they may
have the Father's love as they have ours.

—— LOVING FATHER, ——

We thank You for the children. Let us not only
provide temporal comforts and things, but also
impart to them knowledge of Your law and
Your grace.

IMAGES

And Adam lived one hundred and thirty years, and begot a son in his own likeness, after his image, and named him Seth.

— Genesis 5:3

We all desire children in our own image. Like most fathers, I felt entitled to an unusually handsome and clever child. In Adam's case, this meant more than a boy that looked like his daddy. It meant that Seth had the mark of physical and spiritual death upon him. Similarly, we are all in Seth's image. If we are ever to have life, we must have it from the fountain of life. Christ said, "I am the life."

——— IMMUTABLE FATHER, ———

We thank You for our children. We ask that there will be added to our physical family, those born from above in the image of God.

April

CHANGES

... with whom there is no variation or shadow of turning.

—James 1:17

People our age do not like change. I frown awfully when my place at the table is set with a three-tined fork. Everyone should know that I am used to four tines. Sundays will find me in the same pew. I insist that the grass in my yard be cut on the bias. Sameness is comfortable. I like predictability. How good then to know that the Father does not change. His goodness endures forever.

——— CHANGELESS LORD, ———

When the wind and weather have worn Mount Everest to the ground, You will be the same. In our world, when everything is in a state of change, we praise You for Your constancy.

SPRINGTIME REFLECTIONS

...then I will give you rain in its season, the land shall yield its produce, and the trees of the field shall yield their fruit.

—Leviticus 26:4

I think that the very nature of farming causes the sun-roughened face to turn upward. One can do all that is required by way of preparation, but if the rains do not come, it is for nothing. So it is with all who would sow the Word. We may witness and we may pray, but only God can bring forth the fruit of repentance. When we have done our duty, we may leave the results with God.

——— LORD OF THE HARVEST, ———

We know that we have a deep obligation to plow and to sow, but we recognize that salvation is of the Lord. We thank You for that.

EASTER REFLECTIONS

Because I live, you will live also.
—John 14:19

With the passage of years, the cemetery has become a familiar place to me. Mother, father, nieces, and nephews have been gathered out of my sight from that place. Death leaves a wound that never entirely heals in this lifetime. Long years and many tears have not effaced the memories, nor have they dimmed the love. What joy then, to know that I will see those who are dead in Christ again—because He lives.

——— LOVING FATHER, ———

It gives us joy to now that You will raise us to a different life than we have known. No sin will enter there. We shall have new bodies perfectly fitted to serve You.

FATHERS

"No one can come to Me unless the Father who sent Me draws him ..."

—John 6:44

Though the memory fades with the years, nevertheless I can still hear my fathers call. When he would seek to draw me to him it was not merely an invitation—it was a command! It was never so plain to me that I was his son as when I heard his voice. What a great grace that our Heavenly Father should call us from darkness into His marvelous light. Having drawn me near, He will never let me go!

——— HEAVENLY FATHER, ———

The days are long now since we've heard their voices. They have been long at rest with You. Give us a glimpse of our heavenly home, so that we may have new joy for our journey.

GRIEF

Jesus wept.

—John 11:35

We are encouraged when we read this verse. Lazarus is dead. His sisters Mary and Martha loved him dearly, and their hearts are riven at this profound loss. The multitude that has come to mourn for their departed friend stirs the dust of the burying ground. Jesus beholds this and He weeps. Why does this encourage? It is because He has tasted our sorrows and is acquainted with our grief. He understands when we pray.

———— COMPASSIONATE SAVIOR, ————

We are comforted in our sorrows by knowing that Your heart is also touched. You have tasted all the forms of our grief before us. You understand. Just meditating on that helps.

A FULL QUIVER

So the woman conceived and bore a son. And when she saw that he was a beautiful child, she hid him three months.

—Exodus 2:2

Our youngest grandchild is visiting today. Only seven months old, his mother will not comb his hair for fear that he will lose his baby look. Blondish threadlike filaments stand out from his head as though he were the object of a static electricity experiment. Still, we find him surpassingly handsome. We pray that God will use him as He used the baby Moses to bless His children. Let us, as grandparents, strive to bend their little hearts toward the Father.

——— KINDLY FATHER, ———

We thank You for the children. Please build a fence around them and keep them from the stranger's way. Let them be like Moses, leading many into Your grace.

CELEBRATION

My flesh and my heart fail; but God is the strength of my heart and my portion forever.

—Psalms 73:26

We celebrate our luxuries, our spouses, our health, and our hopes, but when did we last pause to celebrate our inheritance in Jesus Christ? Our riches may drain away. Health may fade. Relationships may wither, and friendships grow cold. But, He is forever unchanging and unchangeable. No words can describe, nor can any mind imagine the wonderful things reserved for us in Him. The thought brings a quiet peace today and presages a glittering tomorrow.

——— ABUNDANT SAVIOR, ———

We would reserve the best of our love for You, but we are also grateful for all that we have in You. These are riches that will not tarnish, nor vanish in time.

EASTER REFLECTIONS

Then, the same day at evening, being the first day of the week, when the doors were shut where the disciples were assembled, for fear of the Jews, Jesus came and stood in the midst, and said to them, "Peace be with you."
—John 20:19

The disciples were defeated. They had left their old lives and livelihoods. Their reputations among their countrymen had been irreparably destroyed. The One on whom they had staked everything lay in a new-made tomb. The Jews, still jeering in the approaching night, might have, at any moment, demanded their sacrifice also. Into this scene stepped the risen Savior and spoke peace to their souls. Let the fact of Christ's resurrection bathe your troubled spirit in an unspeakable, and unfathomable serenity.

——— PRINCE OF PEACE, ———

There is so much about us that causes disquiet. We have no place in this world, and sensing that we are mere pilgrims, many seek our departure. Our only peace is in You.

GLEANING

So Ruth the Moabitess said to Naomi, "Please let me go to the field, and glean heads of grain after him in whose sight I may find favor." And she said to her, "Go, my daughter."
—Ruth 2:2

Ruth is in a hard place. She is a widow and a stranger in Israel. These fields are not hers. She will glean or she will die. Perhaps her redeemer will notice her and be kind. We were much like Ruth. We had no claim to the rich, life-giving grace of God. We were not His people. How could He condescend to notice us? What love is this that causes Him to take us in?

——— BOUNTIFUL LORD, ———

We do not count it a reproach to be gleaners. Your table is rich, and even the crumbs are extravagant as compared to that of our old life. Feed us, lest we die.

SPRINGTIME REFLECTIONS

And there will be a tabernacle for shade in the
daytime from the heat, for a place of refuge,
and for a shelter from storm and rain.

—Isaiah 4:6

God is so good to us. He has provided so
many simple pleasures that even the
least of us can enjoy. I have now experienced
most of life, but I have found few things that
quiet the spirit so much as relishing a spring
rain from the dry comfort of an open porch.
Being blessed with a tin roof to enhance the
sound is a plus. The Lord not only provides our
needs, but also lots of extras.

—— BOUNTIFUL LORD, ——

We are not worthy of the least of Your favors.
Yet, You lavish Your goodness on us. Let us see
Your provision and thank You for it.

EASTER REFLECTIONS

Then he bought fine linen, took Him down, and wrapped Him in the linen. And he laid Him in a tomb which had been hewn out of the rock, and rolled a stone against the door of the tomb.

—Mark 15:46

There is nothing in life that troubles us so much as the prospect of its end. The Christian need have no fear of the cold tomb. The same Lord who has preceded us in pain and in weakness, has gone before us to the stillness of the grave. The knowledge that He has suffered these things removes the sting of them for us. His victory over death secures the same for us. Because He lives, we shall live also.

—————— LIVING LORD, ——————

We were already dead when You found us. You breathed new life into our souls. But, You have purposed to redeem our bodies also. You will raise us to incorruption.

EASTER REFLECTIONS

And behold, there was a great earthquake; for an angel of the Lord descended from heaven, and came and rolled back the stone from the door, and sat on it.

—Matthew 28:2

There is a subtlety here. We must nevermore think of Christ as being in the weakness of the tomb. The mighty Roman Empire has placed the stone at the mouth of the sepulcher. Note that our risen Lord has all authority in heaven and earth. The angel is not bound by any earthly design, but he sits on the very symbol of worldly might. We will rise from the dead because Christ has risen. No power on earth can prevent that.

——— LORD OF LIFE, ———

We know that all of our ways tend toward the tomb. We should be afraid except that You have been there before us. Because You live, we shall live also.

GLORY

And he said, "Brethren and fathers, listen: The God of glory appeared to our father Abraham when he was in Mesopotamia, before he dwelt in Haran,

—Acts 7:2

God is in Himself, glorious. He is, in Himself, our very great reward. It is as though we might draw near Him in heavenly places, and from some advantaged perspective, see Him as He is. The sight will fill us. It will answer every hope and dream of our celestial person. Our every sense will be sated with His splendor. Returning again throughout eternity, we are, on every occasion, rapt in His beauties, but always finding Him wholly new.

——— BEAUTIFUL SAVIOR, ———

Heavenly things are told to us in signs and pictures. It is because we could not now endure the brightness of Your glory. Hasten the day when we shall see You as You are.

CROWNS

Finally, there is laid up for me the crown of righteousness, which the Lord, the righteous Judge, will give to me on that Day, and not to me only but also to all who have loved His appearing.

—2 Timothy 4:8

Knowing myself as I do, I might sense something amiss here. I do not deserve a crown of righteousness. Yet I read that the Lord Himself, the righteous Judge, shall give it to me. That means it has to be legitimate. Christ's righteousness has been imputed to me. I am not only forgiven in Christ, but am righteous also. My mother-in-law feared that I would never amount to anything. I hope she will be there to see.

——— REWARD AND FRIEND, ———

Let the world take rewards where they find them. It is all vanity, and it will pass away. Let me take my portion in Christ. He is eternal.

LOVE

And this is the condemnation, that the light has come into the world, and men loved darkness rather than light, because their deeds were evil.

—John 3:19

We can never get a grasp on how desperate our situation is until we fully appreciate what it is that we love. We are enamored of the darkness. Like thieves, we withdraw from the light so that our deeds are not seen. Light causes us the greatest discomfort. Christ made His generation so uncomfortable that they put Him to death so that the Light might be extinguished. Pray for grace to see yourself as you are.

——— LOVING SAVIOR, ———

We were lost. Though we thought the darkness about us was so thick that we had no idea where we were, You found us. We need no longer fear the night.

Homecoming

Now Joshua the son of Nun, the servant of the Lord, died when he was one hundred and ten years old.

—Judges 2:8

Joshua was great in battle and mighty in faith. When the giants intimidated others, he saw the promise of the grapes. He was the oldest man in Israel. He was the last leaf of his generation upon Israel's tree. Be reminded that the old patriarchs could never have been contented with any piece of land—in Canaan or elsewhere. The promise that they sought is the one that Joshua receives here: A home whose Builder and Maker is God.

——— Heavenly Father, ———

The bright lights have dazzled our eyes and our ears have been stung by the blaring music. Content us with Your brightness, and the whisper of Your grace.

EASTER REFLECTIONS

Jesus said to her, "Woman, why are you weeping? Whom are you seeking?"

—John 20:15

There is a rebuke here. The women have risen early and have come with crushed hearts to minister to the broken body of our Lord. The sad truth is that they are weeping and seeking because of their unbelief. Better that they had heeded the Lord's promise. Then, they would have greeted this day with thanksgiving, knowing that He is raised and is no longer among the dead. These are wise words for us also. Be joyful: Christ is risen.

—— RISEN LORD, ——

We go too often to the graveyard. There we bid farewell to those who are close to our hearts. It is a great comfort to know that we will all be raised together in that great day.

EASTER REFLECTIONS

And they said among themselves, "Who will roll away the stone from the door of the tomb for us?"

—Mark 16:3

This is a worthy question. The days hasten by. Our paths, though winding, all tend toward an end. What hope have we when the grave is closed around us? Who will roll away the stone for us? Our still forms, though dormant through a thousand budding Springs, shall not fail to hear the call of our risen Lord. The corruptible shall put on incorruptibility and our mortal bodies shall be raised to immortality.

——— RESURRECTED SAVIOR, ———

We know that the Father caused Your stone to be rolled away. He will do the same for us also. It is because we are in You. He will not leave us in death.

FORGIVENESS

In Him we have redemption through His blood, the forgiveness of sins, according to the riches of His grace.

—Ephesians 1:7

I hope that we never grow so used to our salvation that we forget the awful price that was paid for it. How could He still be just and forgive us? The horrible blow that ought to have fallen on us, fell on Christ. It pleased the Father to crush the Son, that we might see both in peace. The angels desire to peer into the depths of this marvelous grace. We will have an eternity to look, and never see the bottom.

—————— LOVING SAVIOR, ——————

Let us never forget that Your death was substitutionary. The blows that fell on You ought to have fallen on us. Let us spend eternity in expressing our thankfulness.

REPENTANCE

"Therefore bear fruits worthy of repentance,"
—Matthew 3:8

My son endured abuse from a bully down the block for just about an entire summer. Finally, at my urging, he took his stand and the results were very favorable. Victory, however, seemed to have launched the boy on a campaign of retribution which resulted in daily unprovoked drubbings of his erstwhile nemesis. Our repentance is sometimes like that. It's hard to feel remorse when we are still on top. Un-repented sin will whip us in the end.

——— FORGIVING SAVIOR, ———

Give us a clean heart before You. Cause us to seek our sin and to forsake it. Show us Your forgiveness and Your hatred for our evil ways.

SPRINGTIME REFLECTIONS

The flowers appear on the earth; the time of singing has come, and the voice of the turtledove is heard in our land.

—Song of Solomon 2:12

Sometimes I think the only reason that my wife keeps me is so that she will have someone to do the mule work in our garden. I don't understand flowers and I can't learn the bird's names. She does that, and tells me if she thinks I need to know. I do, however, appreciate flowers in spring, and the soft purring voice of the dove. How wonderful must God be, that He has authored all of this beauty and good?

——— BENEVOLENT MASTER, ———

We look upon the fine work of Your hands and we are amazed. Beauties flow from You, as streams from a mountain snow. Help us to love You more.

OBEDIENCE

"If you love Me, keep My commandments."
—John 14:15

Here is a litmus test for the professing believer. If we would reckon ourselves as children of God, then we must also be obedient to His commands. We live in a very confused era, where many are loath to yield any of their supposed freedoms. The idea of being obedient to parents, or government is energetically resisted. There is no peace for the soul in rebellion. If we are His children, we will obey Him.

——— PATIENT FATHER, ———

Your grace found us as rebels. Help us to remember the misery that this brought to ourselves and to others. We praise You for bringing peace to our souls.

GIVING

...and He saw also a certain poor widow putting in two mites.

—Luke 21:2

We are used to the rich grabbing the headlines. Their gifts draw the attention and admiration of men. The gospel does not set a premium on quantity. That is one reason that it so mightily offends the haughty. Good religion is ever a matter of quality. It is a measure of the heart. Here, the field is truly level. Only that gift tendered by a lowly and humble heart is received and honored by the Father.

—— ACCEPTING FATHER, ——

Accept this small mite of praise. It is small, but it is from the heart. Let others bring riches. Be pleased, we pray, with our humble adoration.

HOLINESS

Pursue peace with all people, and holiness, without which no one will see the Lord:
—Hebrews 12:14

We live in an era when men are in pursuit. Life viewed as a competition is often contrary to amicable relations among people. If we must choose between loss and peace we must choose peace. There can be no true accord with men unless we have harmony with God. The pulpits of our day are almost silent on the subject of holiness. In this, they fail both the ministry and the sinner. Without holiness, no man can see the Lord.

——— HOLY FATHER, ———

Give us a thirst for holiness. You have destined us to be conformed to Your image. Let us be swift then to shed our rags of sin.

EASTER REFLECTIONS

"He is not here, but is risen!"
—Luke 24:6

There is much here to cause excitement! Christ was laid in a new made tomb because our sin pursued Him to the death. But, now He is risen. Ask yourself, "What happened to my sin?" When the answer comes, it will comfort every fear and lighten every burden. It is gone! Gone! Gone! Because our sin was laid on Him, it cannot ever again be reckoned against us. Take that thought to your pillow tonight!

—— GREAT SAVIOR, ——

It is all mystery. We had no home and no hope. Your justice hung over us like a shroud. Only You could deliver us from hell and from the grave.

RETIREMENT

Can two walk together, unless they are agreed?

—AMOS 3:3

Retirement has its special problems. One of them is potentially major and it is completely unexpected. Can it be that we have enjoyed years of marital bliss based on the fact that we used to spend most of the day apart from one another? Two persons living in the same house without children can see an awful lot of each other. It is good that Christ dwells with us. We never tire of knowing Him, or of His care.

—— FATHER OF OUR REST, ——

We thank You for the life partners that You have provided. Help us to have our fellowship in You. That relationship touches all others and fills all with Your love.

CLUTTER

"Therefore I also said, 'I will not drive them out before you; but they shall be thorns in your side, and their gods shall be a snare to you.'"
—Judges 2:3

Israel might have had all the land of Canaan by merely being willing to fight for it. Similarly, we might have conquered all of our inheritance in Christ through an inclination to battle the sin within us. But, we have not. Therefore, we have these thorns in our lives. They add to our sorrows, complicate our relationships with others, and weaken our love for God. They are clutter. We will stumble about until we rid our lives of it.

——— WISE FATHER, ———

We thank You for the tribulation in our lives. We know that You intend good for us. These trials are made for us that they might turn us to a closer walk with You.

JOY

For His anger is but for a moment, his favor
is for life; weeping may endure for a night,
but joy comes in the morning.

—Psalms 30:5

I am but a finite creature, yet I often offend an infinite God. It ought to be that His frown upon me should be forever. But my experience has shown that His anger with me passes. Through the long night, I have wept and mourned because of my sin. The forgiveness of Christ brings joy in the morning. A day will dawn soon that I shall greet in the purity of Christ. Then I will weep no more.

——— FOUNTAIN OF ALL JOYS, ———

The joys that we find in You are not those of the theater or amusement part. They are lasting, satisfying, and eternal.

IGNORANCE

"Yet I have reserved seven thousand in Israel, all whose knees have not bowed to Baal, and every mouth that has not kissed him."

—1 Kings 19:18

Elijah is like a lot of Christians. He feels alone in this world. He thinks that the entire program of God depends on his effort. He is a one-man pity party. We need to be encouraged by the Lord's response to His servant's complaint. We are not alone in the work of the Lord. Neither does success depend on us. It is God that sustains us. He has yet an army of saints who are not defiled by sin and error.

——— OMNISCIENT FATHER, ———

Open our eyes that we may see the work of Your grace around us. Cause us to rejoice that we are many, and that You are much.

SPRINGTIME REFLECTIONS

"If a bird's nest happens to be before you along the way, in any tree or on the ground, with young ones or eggs, with the mother sitting on the young or on the eggs, you shall not take the mother with the young;"

—Deuteronomy 22:6

We have a magnolia by our front door. Often, a pair of birds will build a nest there. Sometimes a cowbird (my wife tells me that this is its name) will come and chase the parent birds away. Then it will kill the young and possess the nest. This marauder loves to live on the labor of others. It is this way with sin. If God does not protect us, it will ruin us—emptying us of everything dear.

——— PRESERVING LORD, ———
We hang by such a slender thread. If You do not protect us, who will be our savior? Gather us under Your wings and shelter us there from danger.

May

1. Love
2. Springtime Reflections
3. Hope
4. Mothers
5. Mothers
6. Mothers
7. Mothers
8. Mothers
9. Mothers
10. Homecoming
11. A Full Quiver
12. Endings
13. Forgiveness
14. Parting
15. Servanthood
16. Brothers and Sisters
17. Simplification
18. Fellowship
19. Faith
20. Ignorance
21. Relationships
22. Ties That Bind
23. Clutter
24. Triumph
25. Joy
26. Obedience
27. Servanthood
28. Values
29. Parting
30. Triumph
31. Relationships

LOVE

A new commandment I give to you, that you love one another; as I have loved you, that you also love one another.

—John 13:34

My mother used to handle the mundane discipline in our home. In the realm of correction, my father was the nuclear cannon. When we heard the words, "Wait until your father gets home," it filled us with fear and foreboding. I'm not sure how often this happens in the present day, but when I misbehaved, my father used to send me out for a switch. He did that because he loved me. Sometimes Christ loves us like that.

——— LOVING SAVIOR, ———

We are glad for the discipline of the Lord. By it, You prove Your love for us. We thank You that You are teaching us how to behave.

SPRINGTIME REFLECTIONS

I sink in deep mire, where there is no standing;
I have come into deep waters, where the floods
overflow me.

—Psalms 69:2

I live in the Midwest. We don't get much in the way of forest fires. Earthquakes are stuff of the newspapers. What we do have plenty of is mud. Springtime brings that. I remember coming home one day with bare feet because the mire had sucked off my shoes. Life is full of muck and mire. It slows us down, blinds our eyes, and makes us dirty. Only God can clean us up and set our feet on solid ground.

——— HOLY GOD, ———

What grace that You should notice our sad situation and provide a remedy for us. Christ has traveled down the same muddy paths as we. Yet, He was without spot or stain.

HOPE

Therefore my heart is glad, and my glory rejoices; my flesh also will rest in hope.

—Psalms 16:9

We know that there is hope for the soul that trusts Jesus Christ. This verse tells us that there is hope for the body also. It is not regenerate today as is our soul. Therefore it must die and be consigned to the grave. But Christ has redeemed us in our entirety—body and soul! Some day it will be raised. We don't know exactly what it will be, but we know that it will be like His glorious body.

—— OUR HOPE AND OUR SALVATION, ——

Today our flesh is our greatest enemy. Nevertheless, we love it, and are eager for the day when it will be made new. Lord, hasten that day.

MOTHERS

And Adam called his wife's name Eve, because she was the mother of all living.

—Genesis 3:20

Our mother Eve certainly had a marvelous life. She was fashioned directly by the hand of God, and was placed in a perfect place under ideal conditions. But, she has known sorrow also. One son was murdered, and another the perpetrator. Every man and woman born down through the millennia are her children. Remember also that Christ is descended from her.

———— HEAVENLY FATHER, ————
We thank You for the work of creation. You are the fountain from which flows every beauty. We thank You for mothers who would lead us to God.

MOTHERS

*My son, hear the instruction of your father,
and do not forsake the law of your mother;*
—Proverbs 1:8

My mother knew some things that helped her immeasurably in the raising of children. She knew that she was the boss, and she knew that the children weren't. She had rules that were Bible based. If the kids entertained any hope of living in peace under her roof, they understood that they must abide by her law. If a child will not submit to the rule of mothers they will never submit to the rule of God.

——— HEAVENLY FATHER, ———

We thank You for godly mothers who feed us with spiritual food. Help us to be loving parents who will lead our children to heaven.

MOTHERS

When I was my father's son, tender and the only one in the sight of my mother,
—Proverbs 4:3

I hope that many of you have fond memories of your mother. Most of us have been buffeted by the world, and in that process we have learned that most people will not love us as our mothers loved us. There is a sense in which Christ is like a mother to His children. He watches them with an eye of love, and corrects them with a stern discipline. Thank the Lord for godly mothers.

——— HEAVENLY FATHER, ———

If our mothers have passed over the Jordan, let us honor them by keeping Your law. If they remain, let us bless them face-to-face.

MOTHERS

Train up a child in the way he should go, and when he is old he will not depart from it.
—Proverbs 22:6

My mother's teaching goes beyond the need for a washed face and brushed teeth. She taught me my obligation to both God and man. There have been times when I found myself in places that I should not be, with people that I ought not to have been with, doing things that I knew better than to do. In these instances, it was my mother's lessons that I recalled. The memory of her words would turn me again into the right way.

——— HEAVENLY FATHER, ———

Turn us again into the godly path given to us by loving mothers. Let us never stray beyond the memory of her instruction.

MOTHERS

For God commanded, saying, 'Honor your father and your mother'; and, 'He who curses father or mother, let him be put to death.'
—Matthew 15:4

It is a sadness that my mother died before very much of life's bounty came to me. I would have enjoyed lavishing her with a measure of the blessings that God poured out on me. She might have liked that, but the thing that would please most is that I have honored the godly instruction that she gave to me. As her eye continues to follow me, I hope she is pleased to find me still in the way.

——— HEAVENLY FATHER, ———
As we are fathers and mothers, let us strive to deserve the honor that You command upon us. Cause us to walk uprightly, and to honor the memory of our own parents.

MOTHERS

Then Abraham breathed his last and died in a good old age, an old man and full of years, and was gathered to his people.

—Genesis 25:8

As the years pass, this verse and others like it grow increasingly dear to me. I long to see the old and dear faces again. I have a growing desire to be "gathered." My Lord will greet me, for I know that my homecoming is precious to Him. My mother will also be there, and I shall know her. Not in the pain and weakness that attended our parting, but in the robustness of eternal health.

——— HEAVENLY FATHER, ———

We have been long parted, but memories of our godly mothers are still fresh upon our minds. We thank You for them, and the promise that we shall see them again soon.

HOMECOMING

Then he charged them and said to them: "I am to be gathered to my people; bury me with my fathers in the cave that is in the field of Ephron the Hittite..."

—Genesis 49:29

There is a beautiful dignity here. Jacob is Israel. He is a prince with God. So many will trace their lineage from him. But, now the sand drains from the glass and Jacob must mark an end. One can almost sense Abraham and Isaac as they begin to make their ways to heaven's gate. Jacob is almost home. Though body and soul approach a divide, each will in its own way obtain the Promised Land by the promise of God.

———— HEAVENLY FATHER, ————

The journey has been long. In the distance, we begin to see the lights of home. How good that You keep them burning for us.

A FULL QUIVER

But Jesus said, "Let the little children come to Me, and do not forbid them; for of such is the kingdom of heaven."

—Matthew 19:14

We have no greater responsibility as parents and grandparents than to assist our little ones in coming to Jesus. Let us do this by both word and deed. Speak lovingly and respectfully of the Lord. By every act, show your submission to His laws and precepts. And by doing so, you will encourage them to come and seek mercy for themselves. We have these blessed assurances that the Savior will both welcome them into His love, and usher them into His Kingdom.

——— LOVING FATHER, ———

Help us to feel that great responsibility of our influence on our families. If they go astray, let it be in spite of us, and not because we have failed in faithfulness.

Endings

> But the day of the Lord will come as a thief in the night, in which the heavens will pass away with a great noise, and the elements will melt with fervent heat; both the earth and the works that are in it will be burned up.
>
> —2 Peter 3:10

Here is both a revelation and a warning. If we plant our roots too deep, and if we love our things too much, we are certain to run upon the reef of disappointment. Houses, lands, people, relationships, everything on the horizon, and the horizon itself is destined for destruction. Lay up treasure in heaven where your investment is as secure as God is eternal. Take your everlasting portion in Christ, or watch your world go up in smoke.

——— Precious Father, ———

You are the only treasure worth seeking. Train our ways so that we expend ourselves in the pursuit of that which cannot pass away.

FORGIVENESS

"Take heed to yourselves. If your brother sins against you, rebuke him; and if he repents, forgive him."

—Luke 17:3

We know ourselves better than any other can know us. When, on the basis of that knowledge, we consider how much Christ has forgiven us, how can we not pardon another? Consider, also, that He atoned for us, while we were yet enemies. Shall we not absolve a brother or sister who asks for restoration? The weight of old grudges is heavy. Let us allow the model of God's free grace to lighten our load.

FORGIVING FRIEND,

Cause us to examine ourselves, and root out the sin that remains in us. Help us also to aid our brothers and sisters so that none miss the high calling of Christ.

PARTING

For sin shall not have dominion over you, for you are not under law but under grace.

—Romans 6:14

Like the children of Israel, we are wont to forget the harshness of our former enslavement. Sin drove us and inflicted every cruelty upon us. It would have seen us in hell except that grace reached out to us. We have made a parting from old ways, and we have entered into the freedom of Christ. Satan shall never again reign over us. Shame on us then, if we should desire to renew our old acquaintance.

——— KINDLY LORD, ———

Help us to greet the day as free men and women. The shackles have been lifted from us. We are no longer bound to former evils. Let us find joy in this truth.

SERVANTHOOD

"And the vinedressers took his servants, beat one, killed one, and stoned another."

—Matthew 21:35

Sometimes the fate of servants is not kind in this world. In this parable of our Lord, He sends servants to receive the fruit of His vineyard, but they are misused and slain. History is replete with variations on this theme. Servants are, however, not fools to forfeit their lives in the Lord's service. They cannot keep their lives forever, in any case. The reaper eventually claims us all. But, the wages of faithfulness are eternal.

——— LOVING MASTER, ———

Our lives can have no better or nobler end than to be used up in Your service. We thank You that You have promised to reward our mortality with immortality.

BROTHERS AND SISTERS

"For whoever does the will of God is My brother and My sister and mother."

—Mark 3:35

There is much mystery here, but our life experience affirms this truth. When we are far from home, how often does the name of Jesus find for us a brother or sister? When language is a barrier and custom divides us, does not our kinship in Christ unite us? Love and obedience to our Lord kindles the sweetest affection within the family.

 LOVING FATHER,

We thank You for the family of God. When we think our road would be too long for us, You send a brother or sister to come along side and offer us a cool drink of water along the way.

SIMPLIFICATION

And the Lord said to Gideon, "The people who are with you are too many for Me to give the Midianites into their hands, lest Israel claim glory for itself against Me, saying, 'My own hand has saved me.'"

—Judges 7:2

We are wont to trust in the wrong things. If we have a talent, the tendency is to rely on that. Money will seduce the soul and cause a false confidence in riches. Gideon had too many men. He had a need to thin things out and to simplify. How often have we credited the victory to some strength other than God? In this, we rob Him of glory, and we bring a harmful delusion upon ourselves.

—— O GOD OUR STRENGTH, ——

Take from us our delusions. We are prone to trust in ourselves, and to attribute our triumphs to the wrong things. Help us to see that You are our strength and salvation.

FELLOWSHIP

...that which we have seen and heard we declare to you, that you also may have fellowship with us; and truly our fellowship is with the Father and with His Son Jesus Christ.

—1 John 1:3

Paul tells us in Romans that the natural man is at enmity with God. How then, can it be that we have fellowship with the Father? It is because we have become sons and daughters through Jesus Christ. He has revealed the Father to us. He has made us just and righteous so that God can condescend to talk with us, and give to us the desires of our regenerate hearts. Not just for now, but for eternity!

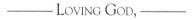

—— LOVING GOD, ——

We who were once enemies have been subdued by Your grace and adopted into Your family. Help us to see the honor of our standing, and to seek to be worthy of it.

FAITH

"Now if God so clothes the grass of the field, which today is, and tomorrow is thrown into the oven, will He not much more clothe you, O you of little faith?"

—Matthew 6:30

I don't think we ponder much about the outrage of little faith. To have faith is to believe God. God has made all things. He keeps them working by the word of His power. We shall not have our next breath unless He grants it to us. How then, do we have the effrontery to disbelieve Him? It is glorifying to the Father that He is patient with us. Where we are weak, He gives us faith.

——— PATIENT PROVIDER, ———

Having given us Your only Son, what will You then withhold? Teach us to trust in Your provision. There is no bottom to Your treasures.

IGNORANCE

"All that the Father gives Me will come to Me, and the one who comes to Me I will by no means cast out."

—John 6:37

My uncles would sit on the tailgates of their old pickup trucks and sip their "white lightening." At some point, they would inevitably wax theological. Each would spend some conversation in assuring the others that they all were among God's elect. I hope that their certitude was warranted, but I fear that it was ignorance speaking. It is sure that all of the elect will come to Christ, but if we have not come, we have no basis for assurance.

—— OMNISCIENT FATHER, ——

We praise You that we have come to You and You have not turned us away. You have set Your love upon us and You will not let us go.

RELATIONSHIPS

Therefore, whether you eat or drink, or whatever you do, do all to the glory of God.
—1 Corinthians 10:31

I haven't always had the good sense that I ought to have had. My foolishness has led me to make friends that I would have been better off without. In this matter, as in all others, our aim should be the glory of God. Companions that take us where we ought not to go tarnish us. Comrades, whose speech is not pure, pollute us. Let us examine the roster of our friendships with an eye toward the glory of God.

——— DEAR FATHER, ———
We thank You for the friends that You have brought in our paths. Cause us to be patient with one-another, and to mutually perfect our walk with You.

TIES THAT BIND

"Therefore know that the Lord your God, He is God, the faithful God who keeps covenant and mercy for a thousand generations with those who love Him and keep His commandments;"
—Deuteronomy 7:9

We are bound to the Lord by a covenant of grace. He is faithful to do all that He has pledged. It is a good thing, because we are inconstant in our affections and unsteady in our purposes. He is pleased to continue to show us mercy, because He sees us as we are in Christ. We obey Him because we adore and fear Him. When the world has passed away, we will still be bound to Christ in love.

——— FAITHFUL FATHER, ———

Had You not loved us, what would be our end? We were in darkness and would never have desired the light. You sought us in our ruin and made us children. We love You for that.

CLUTTER

"...and the cares of this world, the deceitfulness of riches, and the desires for other things entering in choke the word, and it becomes unfruitful.

—Mark 4:19

That one who makes worldly pleasure, peace, or wealth his primary objective will neither please God nor achieve his goals. These things are clutter that obscure our light and block our way. We are deceived when we desire temporal pleasures above eternal treasures. It is only as we love the Father and do our duty to Him that we obtain the riches of Christ. How peaceful is the sleep of that one whose affection is fixed upon God!

——— OMNISCIENT FATHER, ———

You have made us, and You are the only one who can fully fill our void of longing. Show Christ to our souls that we may be full for time, and for eternity.

TRIUMPH

Then the priests who bore the ark of the covenant of the Lord stood firm on dry ground in the midst of the Jordan; and all Israel crossed over on dry ground, until all the people had crossed completely over the Jordan.

—Joshua 3:17

It seemed a very unlikely thing. These are a slave people who worked the brick ovens of Egypt in the hot sun. Weak and ravaged by their oppressors, all that they had in the way of assets was the avowal of God. Confounding every probability, they stand now upon the very object of the promise. Note particularly that everyone who was heir to the promise passed over in Canaan. So shall He bring all His people into rest.

——— FAITHFUL FATHER, ———

We are foolish and sometimes circumstances of the day cause doubts to arise in our minds. Quiet our fears with a renewed confidence in Your faithfulness.

JOY

Those who sow in tears shall reap in joy.
—Psalms 126:5

Some Christians will leave the field upon the smallest injury. We have many causes for tears. But, this is not sufficient reason to cease sowing. This we must do, though the tears fall like summer rain. We know that a harvest time is before us. In that day, we shall bountifully reap the seeds that we have sown. Then the sorrows of past times will be a memory, and the joy before us without end.

——— FOUNTAIN OF ALL JOYS, ———
Help us to sow daily the seed of righteousness and good works. Let the day come soon when we shall see the harvest by Your grace.

OBEDIENCE

"Now therefore, if you will indeed obey My voice and keep My covenant, then you shall be a special treasure to Me above all people; for all the earth is Mine."

—Exodus 19:5

God is our creator. He has made all men. How preposterous it is that all men should not obey Him. While, in a sense, there is value in all, those who obey the Lord are particularly precious. We are often disobedient to God so that we may please another. How foolish! When this entire world has been reduced to cinders, He will remain. In that day, He will gather His treasure near. No place will be found for the disobedient.

———— DEAR LORD, ————

Who would change the Lord? Who would alter Your perfections? Let us not rebel against You. Let us trust You and obey.

SERVANTHOOD

"So those servants went out into the highways and gathered together all whom they found, both bad and good. And the wedding hall was filled with guests."

—Matthew 22:10

These servants are gathering guests for a great wedding feast. Note that it is not in the purview of the servant to select the attendees. Any that they meet are candidates. Some meet a high standard and others fail this test. But, all may come any many do. It is the servant's job to announce, and invite. It is humble work. The reward will come when every seat is filled, and the king's purpose is accomplished.

——— GRACIOUS KING, ———

We are glad that we are also invited to the great feast. We thank You for the joy that we shall know when we arrive bringing a host with us.

VALUES

He who says, "I know Him," and does not keep His commandments, is a liar, and the truth is not in him.

—1 John 2:4

I t is a hypocritical time. We have degenerated so far in this area that people do not even expect that the person speaking is sincere in what they say. Everything is a matter of spin. We wind up hoping that what we are told is at least approximately true. We will all some day come into a judgment where God will demand and reveal truth in clear and precise terms. No man will stand in that hour without the Truth.

——— BLESSED TRUTH, ———

Cleanse our lying mouths and give us revulsion for the lie. Press Your commandments to our hearts, and help us to love Your ways.

PARTING

But God forbid that I should boast except in the cross of our Lord Jesus Christ, by whom the world has been crucified to me, and I to the world.

—Galatians 6:14

Paul is here illuminating a fact of the Christian life. It is a threshold beyond which there is a mutual recognition of a most unique occurrence. The world has lost its glitter and glow. The things that once attracted now repel. The emblems of life now reek of death. The world has died to us. It is by mutual consent. The world views us as dead. We are parted. By grace, we can never again be reconciled.

——— KINDLY LORD, ———

The world is dead to us. It has lost its former attraction. You have turned our affections to higher things. We praise You for that.

TRIUMPH

O my God, I trust in You; let me not be ashamed; let not my enemies triumph over me.

—Psalms 25:2

I have my share of enemies. In some instances, Christ is the reason for their malignity. Often, it seems to me that their interests have carried the day. God has been cast from the schoolroom and public life. The world seems an inhospitable place for the God-fearing. I am comforted by this verse. No matter the ebb and flow of daily events, the victory is mine through Christ. If someone must worry tonight, let it be the adversaries of the Lord.

—— O LORD AND PROTECTOR, ——

Our days are long, and they appear to be full of perils. Help us to see Your wall about us. Give us a vision of our final victory where You are all in all.

RELATIONSHIPS

To Timothy, a true son in the faith: Grace, mercy, and peace from God our Father and Jesus Christ our Lord.

—1 Timothy 1:2

I have a lot of relations. Some of them I talk about more than others. I have a suspicion that some of them are just a little reluctant to mention me. There is a group that stand in relationship to me, however, that I am always pleased to mention. They are my sons and daughters in the faith. If I have concerns about them at all, it is that there are too few of them. May their numbers increase.

——— DEAR FATHER, ———

Help us to have zeal in increasing our relations. Let us be about the cultivation of sons and daughters in the faith. Heaven will be the brighter for the presence of family.

June

1. Homecoming
2. Ignorance
3. Repentance
4. Experience
5. Parting
6. Celebration
7. Moving
8. Passing It On
9. Values
10. Glory
11. Fellowship
12. Fathers
13. Fathers
14. Fathers
15. Fathers
16. Fathers
17. Fathers
18. Glory
19. Changes
20. Beginnings
21. Simplification
22. Endings
23. Values
24. Faith
25. Changes
26. Giving
27. Brothers and Sisters
28. Forgiveness
29. Flexibility
30. Summer Vacations

HOMECOMING

"and die on the mountain which you ascend, and be gathered to your people, just as Aaron your brother died on Mount Hor and was gathered to his people;"

—Deuteronomy 32:50

Moses had been called the son of Pharoah's daughter. He might have run things in that old world except the scripture says that he counted both the cost and reward of serving the Lord. Well, this is reward day. The gold and fame of Egypt are behind. All of God's glory is ahead. Moses did not set one foot in Canaan. He had no abode there. God has made a home for him, however, and he will greet the morning there.

——— HEAVENLY FATHER, ———

We begin to grow a little excited. A fresh breeze lifts our small craft and tends it toward the harbor. We bless You forever for making a place for us there.

IGNORANCE

But I do not want you to be ignorant, brethren, concerning those who have fallen asleep, lest you sorrow as others who have no hope.

—1 Thessalonians 4:13

Over the centuries, a lot of people have died. One supposes that there are more of them than of us. We should not be ignorant concerning them. Those who sleep in Jesus are going to rise again. Should we join this innumerable band soon, it is no small comfort to know that we will not be left to molder. Christ, who has saved us, has done so in our entirety. We shall be with the Lord—body and soul.

—— OMNISCIENT FATHER, ——

We thank You that You have left no part of us to be counted as a casualty of sin. You have redeemed us, and we shall live forever with You in our entirety.

REPENTANCE

For you know that afterward, when he wanted to inherit the blessing, he was rejected, for he found no place for repentance, though he sought it diligently with tears.

—Hebrews 12:17

As a young man, I was driving home from the West coast and stopped for a meal in a Las Vegas restaurant. I turned around and there was one of those ubiquitous slot machines. I thumbed in a dime, and it paid me back about eighty cents. Suddenly I saw no harm in gambling. That is, until it took all the money back—including my original dime. Like Esau I repented—not from real sorrow, but because I had suffered a loss.

——— FORGIVING SAVIOR, ———

Strip away our delusions. Cause us to know Your hatred for sin. Help us to see that it was our sin that nailed You to the cross.

EXPERIENCE

For the wages of sin is death, but the gift of God is eternal life in Christ Jesus our Lord.
—Romans 6:23

Experience has taught us the truth of these words. The stench of ruin hangs about sin as carrion follow death. It brings the demise of self-respect, of maternal and marital love, of responsibility and dependability, and of fidelity and trust. How is it that we can so love that which is unable to love us? The day will be bright and glorious when we bid goodbye to sin, and cleave only to the Father!

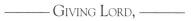 GIVING LORD,

Prompt our souls to consider Your wonderful gift to us. What manner of love is this, which motivates a Father to offer His only Son?

PARTING

For as in Adam all die, even so in Christ all
shall be made alive.

—1 Corinthians 15:22

One penalty of age is that it has drawn us to stand before many a new-made grave. There we have parted from mother and father. Beside the wounded earth, we have marked an end to love and life. The scars ache still and the years never totally efface the hurt. We must blame sin for that. But, we must not forsake the promise secured to us by Christ. The dead shall live again in a land where partings will be unknown.

——— KINDLY LORD, ———

You are not the God of the dead, but of the living. We exit this world to take on a new and more fulfilling life. Help us to brush away the tears and enter into the joy.

CELEBRATION

And He took bread, gave thanks and broke it, and gave it to them, saying, "This is My body which is given for you; do this in remembrance of Me."

—Luke 22:19

The bleating of the Pascal lambs wafts upon a stirring breeze into the Jerusalem night. Our Lord will be surrendered soon into the hands of an inflamed and howling mob. None will stand with Him. Insults and slanders will be heaped upon Him. Thorns will crush His head, and His hands will be pierced by Roman nails. Let us eat the bread and drink the wine in remembrance until we celebrate at last in His arms.

——— SAVING LORD, ———

We can never allow our hearts to travel far from the awful truth that You gave Yourself for us. Let us ponder this truth often, in sober celebration.

MOVING

You are the Lord God, who chose Abram, and brought him out of Ur of the Chaldeans, and gave him the name Abraham;

—Nehemiah 9:7

Moving is a "big deal!" When my wife and I were married, we were still in college. When we moved to our first apartment, everything that we jointly owned fit very nicely into the back seat of our old car. Abram got an entirely new country out of his big move. Someday, the Lord will move us to a new place also. Like Abraham, we will never have a desire to go back to our old home.

——— HEAVENLY FATHER, ———

We are like the caged lion. We know that we were made for better things. Let the restraints be lifted so that we can soar to heaven. We will find a fit home there.

PASSING IT ON

So he departed from there, and found Elisha the son of Shaphat, who was plowing with twelve yoke of oxen before him, and he was with the twelfth. Then Elijah passed by him and threw his mantle on him.

—1 Kings 19:19

See how sovereignly it is done? God does not consult with anyone. He will have the mantle of Elijah fall on Elisha, and it is concluded! It is the call of God. Pity poor Elisha if he does not heed this summons. We have received our faith by the witness of another. There is much to be done, and we are called to do it. Let us be about passing the mantle of truth to others.

——— TRIUMPHANT LORD, ———

We thank You for that One who brought the truth to us. Help us to be the bearer of Your Gospel to others.

VALUES

Children, obey your parents in the Lord, for
this is right.

—Ephesians 6:1

My wife returned from a morning of "baby sitting" some of the children of our church. One might suppose that these youngsters would achieve a higher standard of behavior than kids generally. In some ways, I hope that isn't true. What has happened to the value of obedience? Will a little one obey God if they feel no obligation to the authority of mother and father? Young parents, bring your children into submission—for this is right.

———— PATIENT FATHER, ————

We are embarrassed that we have neglected Your law. Give us a renewed awareness of the seriousness of our obligation to be obedient and to inculcate this into our children.

Glory

For You, Lord, are most high above all the
earth; you are exalted far above all gods.
—Psalms 97:9

Glorifying God involves an appreciation of Him. We must acknowledge in our hearts that He has made us. Every breath of our long lives has come from Him. He has built a protective hedge around us, freely provided for our every need, and has strewn our paths with bounty and goodness. Mercy and grace are ours by His design. He has given us His only Son. Eternity we will be insufficient to exhaust our admiration of Him.

———— Awesome God, ————

We know that You have made us. Forgive us when we fail to acknowledge Your loftiness. Your ways transcend our ways as the stars above the earth.

FELLOWSHIP

And they continued steadfastly in the apostles' doctrine and fellowship, in the breaking of bread, and in prayers.

—Acts 2:42

Fellowship among Christians is not akin to that found in the beer halls and gambling dens. It is not that which extends to any unbelieving heart—no matter how close they are by blood or affection. It is a union of souls that has at its center Truth, which is in Jesus Christ. Whom He loved, He loved until the end. So, as long as we have life and breath, we are bonded to one another in the Truth.

———— HEAVENLY FATHER, ————

We thank You for Your large family. We expect to have eternity to get to know them. Let us love each one that we meet here as You have loved them.

FATHERS

"Look at the birds of the air, for they neither sow nor reap nor gather into barns; yet your heavenly Father feeds them. Are you not of more value than they?"

—Matthew 6:26

To say that my father fed us would be a gross understatement. We were a farm family transported to the city. The size of breakfast would have been appropriate had we just emerged from labors in the field, instead of hours in the bed. He grew some big boys! Similarly, my Heavenly Father has fed me all my life. He has done this a day at a time. It has always been more than I deserved or expected.

——— FAITHFUL PROVIDER, ———

Daily, we have come to You, and You have not failed to feed us. Give us also that heavenly manna that we may be full of Your choicest blessings.

FATHERS

Therefore it is of faith that it might be according to grace, so that the promise might be sure to all the seed, not only to those who are of the law, but also to those who are of the faith of Abraham, who is the father of us all.

—Romans 4:16

Abraham was the father of "many nations." This was so in the fleshly sense, but it is also true in the spiritual. He heard the call of God and believed when he was among the idolaters of Ur. Drawn from the familiar, and the comfort of family, he sought a land and an inheritance that he had never seen. He is "father" of all of the faithful, and we are pleased to call him ours.

——— FAITHFUL FATHER, ———

Abraham saw Your day and he was glad. We also have seen You and we will never be the same. Help us to return Your faithfulness. Help us to love You more.

FATHERS

And because you are sons, God has sent forth the Spirit of His Son into your hearts, crying out, "Abba, Father!"

—Galatians 4:6

I am at an age where I am sensible to the value of an inheritance. Others in my circle have had the benefit of those, and it seems, from a distance, to have helped them. It's nice to know then that I have an adopted Father who has taken me into a very rich family. All things belong to Him, and He has given all to Christ. My life with Him will never end, and my legacy will never decay.

——— HEAVENLY FATHER, ———

Many of our fathers have gone to sleep in faith. We miss them, but we are so thankful that You have also been our Father. You have been our comfort and our hope.

FATHERS

And Jacob gave Esau bread and stew of lentils;
then he ate and drank, arose, and went his
way. Thus Esau despised his birthright.
—Genesis 25:34

Esau was a loser in this transaction. His eyes were on things, and his thoughts were on his belly. He had no respect for the promise of God: that the Savior would come through his father's line. He is like his modern brother who is inclined to view these things as foolishness. He remains no less the son of his father, but oh, the loss that he is not numbered among the sons of God.

——— PROMISE KEEPER, ———

Keep our eyes off of earthly treasure, and our thoughts from the satisfaction of the flesh. Better that we should spend our days in hunger, than to forfeit our home in glory.

FATHERS

For whom the Lord loves He corrects, just as a father the son in whom he delights.

—Proverbs 3:12

Our generation precedes the "time out" era of child discipline. Our fathers saw no problem with corporal punishment. My father not only whipped me, but allowed me to fetch my own switch. I won't pretend to have enjoyed these "quality times," but from the vantage point of years, I would not have done without them. I am a better man, my love for my dad is deeper, and my memories of him are dearer because of them.

JUST CREATOR,

Help us to search our things in us that displease You. Cause us to forsake these that we might please You more. If not, chastise us so that we may know that we are sons and daughters.

FATHERS

And when Jacob had finished commanding
his sons, he drew his feet up into the bed and
breathed his last, and was gathered to his
people.

—Genesis 49:33

Jacob died in faith. That is a beautiful
and dignified thing. Jacob's family was
notable and blessed. Isaac was his father, and
Abraham his grandfather. But the people to
whom he was gathered were only secondarily
his fleshly kin. They were his brothers and
sisters in the faith. It may be said that these are
our family also. I am eager to be "gathered" to
them—for they are with Christ. There, I also
desire to be.

—— GRACIOUS GATHERER OF SOULS, ——
The day is approaching when we will also be
gathered. Even now we can hear the voices,
and see the faint forms. Hasten the hour of our
homecoming.

GLORY

And having been perfected, He became the author of eternal salvation to all who obey Him,

—Hebrews 5:9

We fool ourselves if we believe that we can glorify God while going our ways in disobedience. Our age is one where scarcely anyone submits to authority. We choke upon some ill-conceived notion of our precious rights. We will not have this One to rule over us. Happiness is ever out of reach of that one who does not defer to God's commands. The Christian obeys God because to disobey robs Him of His great glory.

——— GLORIOUS GOD, ———

You have made more honorable, and nobler creatures than us. We Thank You for allowing such meager ones as we to praise Your wonderful name.

Changes

I have been young, and now am old; Yet I have not seen the righteous forsaken, Nor his descendants begging bread.

—Psalms 37:25

As my father lay upon his deathbed, I noted that he would often stare at his hands. I find myself doing that now. It is as though I cannot grasp the foreboding change written there. I was young and am now old. Yet, I do not face the future alone. He will see me safely home. Moreover, I trust that I leave a legacy of faith to my children. They will not accept poisoned spiritual bread from another.

——— Ageless Father, ———

Increasingly, our generation withers and is carried away. You are ever the same, and some day we will be like You. We praise You for that.

BEGINNINGS

"And the Lord said to me, 'See, I have begun to give Sihon and his land over to you. Begin to possess it, that you may inherit his land.'"
— Deuteronomy 2:31

God has given us a great inheritance through Jesus Christ. Sin is a barrier to our possession of it. The Lord has promised that we can win this battle. He will go before us, but He will not go for us. We must engage the enemy. We cannot do this by other means than to put him to death. If we do not do this, we will live forever in his land, under the torment of his rule.

———— MIGHTY GOD, ————

Give us the desire to root out every evil that we have allowed to remain in our lives. Give us the strength and the weapons to pursue our faults until they are exterminated.

SIMPLIFICATION

He found a fresh jawbone of a donkey, reached out his hand and took it, and killed a thousand men with it.

—Judges 15:15

In an era of "weapons systems" and war by computer chip, we are impressed by the simplicity of Samson's weaponry. What ought to grab our attention and humble our pride is the fact that God can use anything to accomplish His purposes. We are not necessary to the victory, but the Lord is pleased to use weak instruments because His glory shines the more brightly through them. The older we grow, the more grateful to Him we are.

——— HOLY FATHER, ———

We thank You that You condescend to use us as instruments of Your design. Make us humble that we may see, and delight in Your grace.

ENDINGS

A time to be born, and a time to die; a time to plant, and a time to pluck what is planted;
— Ecclesiastes 3:2

What a great grace it is that, though we all know that we must die, we are able to live joyfully. That is because we do not know the hour of our ending. But, God's grace may be abused. Foolish is that person who does not have at least one eye on the actuarial tables. Look around. How many two-hundred-year-olds do you see? Make peace with God today. We may not live to greet tomorrow.

— KINDLY LORD, —

Teach us to live as though this day may be our last. We thank You that though we know this road has an ending, You have strewn it with many joys.

VALUES

For we have spent enough of our past lifetime in doing the will of the Gentiles when we walked in lewdness, lusts, drunkenness, revelries, drinking parties, and abominable idolatries.

—1 Peter 4:3

Lewdness has become a part of our societal fabric. It is prominent in our speech, the focus of our entertainments, the motivation of our advertising, and the catalyst of our soaring divorce statistics. That one who is most obedient to the law of God sleeps best at night. We seem incapable of grasping the fact that the godly life is an inherently superior life. Ask the person who wonders right now just how much their spouse knows.

——— LORD, ———

You have given us Your commandments not only that we may honor You in their keeping, but also that we may lead lives of purity and happiness. Help us to see that.

FAITH

For in it the righteousness of God is revealed from faith to faith; as it is written, "The just shall live by faith."

—Romans 1:17

Every time I encounter this verse it evokes an image that always impresses and uplifts. I see generations of saints passing the torch of faith up through the centuries. Through privation and plenty, in forests and glades, from cathedrals and humble country churches—each hand pressing the torch of our precious faith into the eager grasp of the next. The hour is late. Ought we to be about the task of passing it on?

——— GLORIOUS SAVIOR, ———

We thank You for the instruments of Your grace. We thank You for that One who first told us of Your love and forgiveness.

Changes

Every good gift and every perfect gift is from above, and comes down from the Father of lights, with whom there is no variation or shadow of turning.

—James 1:17

In youth, I thought there were some earthly truths that could be relied upon. I would make my career with a solid company that would be there for me in retirement. I would invest in stocks that would always rise in value. I would rely on laws that always sought justice. What a comfort in this world of disappointing change that I have placed my faith in One in whom there is no variation.

—— Heavenly Father, ——

Where would we anchor our lives if it were not for You? The waves of change beat upon us, but we do not move. For our anchor is sure.

GIVING

"If you then, being evil, know how to give good gifts to your children, how much more will your Father who is in heaven give good things to those who ask Him!"

—Matthew 7:11

When the ice cream man would wend his way through my old neighborhood, my brothers and I would find my father and beg him for dimes. Economic conditions and the standards of the time and place caused it to be a seldom thing that he would grant our request. But, when the coins were forthcoming it was a rich gift indeed! My Heavenly Father knows just what I need. Having already given me His Son, will He withhold any good thing from me?

————— GENEROUS LORD, —————

We cannot buy Your mercy, since then it would not be pardon, but purchase. All things are Yours. You cannot be enriched by the wealth that we hold. Help us to love Your grace.

BROTHERS AND SISTERS

And she had a sister called Mary, who also sat at Jesus' feet and heard His word.

—Luke 10:39

The bond between sisters is one of life's great blessings. There is a closeness and a tenderness that is not observed between any other relations. Only one tie excels it: the cord of adoration that binds us to the Savior. When sisters are content to sit at Jesus' feet, their mutual love is eternal. Our relationship with Christ imbues every other relationship with a beauty that does not diminish with time.

—————— BEAUTIFUL SAVIOR, ——————

We thank You for our sisters. We cannot imagine what life would be like without the gentleness and sweetness that flows from a sister's love.

FORGIVENESS

And forgive us our debts, as we forgive our debtors.

—Matthew 6:12

There is a startling concept here. We, who need so much forgiveness, are to be treated in the same manner as we treat others. That's a very sobering thought. It should motivate us to be active in this business of mercy. It is sad to see folks our age walking around with a hard edge and flinty eye toward those who have done us wrong. We are too near the judgment seat ourselves to withhold pardon from others.

 FORGIVING LORD,

The mountain of our debt was high before us. Who could satisfy the just demands of the Father? You satisfied our indebtedness. Let us not deny forgiveness to others.

FLEXIBILITY

Jesus said to him, "Rise, take up your bed and walk." And immediately the man was made well, took up his bed, and walked.

—John 5:8, 9

This poor man had lain beside the pool of Bethesda for thirty-eight years. Doubtless, he believed that he would finish his pitiful days there. Similarly, we may also be sure that our hopes, and aspirations will never be realized. We will lay here helpless forever! Isn't it better that we remain hopeful? God may just decide to bless us. Stay flexible! Today may be our day! In this life, or the next—things are going to get a lot better!

———— FATHER OF ALL GOODNESS, ————
Who are we to say that we will head for the bench? Let us not forget our servanthood so that we turn to sloth. Cause us to be up and about the business of the Kingdom.

SUMMER VACATIONS

"Have you entered the treasury of snow, or have you seen the treasury of hail,"

—Job 38:22

Some folks head North in summer, seeking the cool and the snow. Personally, I think that snow "keeps" better today than in the past. When it laid around for very long it became sooty. The fact that there were few restrictions on pets then didn't help much either. Snow does not come from a "treasury," but is made, as required, on the spot. So are all of God's providences—made as required for our blessing and His glory.

——— BLESSED CREATOR, ———

We thank You that all of our days You have provided every good thing for us. Refresh us now with Your providence. Let us see in Your creation, Your unsearchable love for us.

July

1. Love
2. Holiness
3. Summer Vacations
4. Homecoming
5. Summer Vacations
6. Experience
7. Grief
8. Gleaning
9. Crowns
10. Changes
11. Hard Work
12. Images
13. Fellowship
14. Joy
15. Love
16. Faith
17. Glory
18. Joy
19. Summer Vacations
20. Harvest Time
21. Waging the Battle
22. Obedience
23. Repentance
24. Flexibility
25. Hope
26. Retirement
27. Ignorance
28. Servanthood
29. Ties That Bind
30. Summer Vacations
31. Triumph

LOVE

Though I speak with the tongues of men and of angels, but have not love, I have become sounding brass or a clanging cymbal.

—1 Corinthians 13:1

The Corinthians seemed to value the gift of eloquence. On this basis, they had contempt for others who were more crude in their expression. Good religion is a matter of the heart. Though we have the gift of a thousand languages, if our hearts do not follow our speech, then our vaunted oratory is discord—mere noise. God will give us real, constant, sacrificial love. That is love of God, which helps men and glorifies God.

—— LOVING SAVIOR, ——

We cannot love as You would have us do, unless we obtain that love from You. We pray that You would shower this upon us so that we might lavish it upon others.

HOLINESS

Because the carnal mind is enmity against God; for it is not subject to the law of God, nor indeed can be.

—Romans 8:7

We can understand from our verse why there is so little discussion of holiness in our day. It is a subject that causes the natural man discomfort. If holiness is pressed upon him, he will shirk. If it is demanded, he will strike. Unless grace should seize him, he will not submit because he cannot submit to the law of God. When you are upon your pillow tonight, pause to thank God that He has given you a desire for holiness.

─────── HOLY FATHER, ───────

Show us that it is love of God that drives out a desire for sin. Show us that we cannot obey You unless we come to Love You.

SUMMER VACATIONS

'And he shall be like the light of the morning when the sun rises, a morning without clouds, like the tender grass springing out of the earth, by clear shining after rain.'

—2 Samuel 23:4

Few things cause as much financial and emotional pain as a rainy vacation. A good tan and recreation are impossible when clouds cover the sun, and water covers everything else. How refreshing when the sun appears in the morning! It portends a good day. Christ is like that to the Christian. Just the thought of Him drives away the concerns and anxieties of the soul. Our hearts desire a morning that never draws on the night.

——— FATHER OF LIGHTS, ———

We thank You for Your faithfulness. Every day the sun rises. Every night brings rest. Fill our waking hours with a sense of Your goodness, and our sleep with dreams of peace.

HOMECOMING

Then it happened, as they continued on and talked, that suddenly a chariot of fire appeared with horses of fire, and separated the two of them; and Elijah went up by a whirlwind into heaven.

—2 Kings 2:11

I have always wanted to enjoy a limousine ride. There have not been many opportunities to do that. The little experience that I have tells me that luxury transportation is for opulent destinations. If this applies to our verse, I would say that it bodes very well for our departing prophet. God has sent a rich ride to bring His servant home. This leads me to believe that our homecoming is intended to be a very big event.

——— HEAVENLY FATHER, ———

We do not know the means of our passing over, nor are we told the time or circumstance. We know that You will be there to comfort us.

SUMMER VACATIONS

The wilderness and the wasteland shall be glad for them, and the desert shall rejoice and blossom as the rose;

—Isaiah 35:1

I remember a summer vacation to the West coast. Our return route took us through Death Valley. The most memorable thing about that experience was the quiet of the place. There was no leaf to rustle, and no wind to stir it. I could hear the beating of my own heart. I think it would be a good thing to check the condition of our hearts often. Hearing the pulse of our mortality would help us listen to the Lord.

——— LORD, ———

For lack of faith, our hearts are often dry. There is no joy or pleasure in our lives. Help us to be full of You that we might blossom and be glad.

JULY 6

EXPERIENCE

"We must through many tribulations enter the kingdom of God."

—Acts 14:22

Every time we reach the crest of one of life's hills, we expect a long, leisurely downward glide. Experience teaches me that what is more likely is that the runner is just about to come off of my sled. Life is like that! My sweet father encapsulated so much wisdom when he said, "Son there's always something." I'm convinced now that it is so for my good. It keeps me from loving this world too much.

——— HEAVENLY FATHER, ———

We thank You for the difficulties that You have sewn into the fabric of our days. They mature us in the faith. Trials make us long for heaven.

GRIEF

...sorrowing most of all for the words which he spoke, that they would see his face no more. And they accompanied him to the ship.

—Acts 20:38

Life is full of these tender moments. At our age, we cannot forbear thinking, as we take our leave of loved ones, that we may never see them again. Experience prompts this for our hearts already have a hundred empty places. Paul will never see these elders again in this world. Think though, of that great reunion morning when we shall meet again at the feet of the Savior. There will be no grief of parting there.

—— UNDERSTANDING LORD, ——

We thank You that we do not sorrow as those who have no hope. Because You are raised, we shall rise also. Death is swallowed up in victory.

GLEANING

So Mephibosheth dwelt in Jerusalem, for he ate continually at the king's table. And he was lame in both his feet.

—2 Samuel 9:13

This was so much more than Mephibosheth could have expected. No one would have questioned had he been put to death. He was crippled and of a cursed lineage—the natural enemy of the king. He would have counted it all grace had he been merely granted opportunity to glean the crumbs falling from David's table. Mercy will cause him to dine with the king's sons. The white cloth spread to receive his lord's bounty will hide his lameness.

——— MERCIFUL FATHER, ———

We are so like Mephibosheth. We were servants of another master. We were enemies of God. But You desired to show us mercy. Now we dine at the King's table.

CROWNS

...and when the Chief Shepherd appears, you will receive the crown of glory that does not fade away.

—1 Peter 5:4

It has bothered me a little, over the years, that everyone doesn't appreciate me as they should. Being a little bald and pudgy hasn't helped. It is a comfort to realize that I am destined for better things. I will be crowned with a glorious crown. Not for what I have accomplished in myself, but for what Christ has done for me. Such few symbols of recognition as I have received are faded with the years. I await a crown eternal.

——— GLORIOUS FATHER, ———

The heavens declare Your glory. You are like the stars that shine eternally in the heavens. Our rewards in Your service will also shine forever.

CHANGES

They immediately left their nets and followed Him.

—Matthew 4:20

Peter and Andrew had been fishermen. Doubtless that they had made plans for this day. But grace had designs also. Someone would have to show flexibility. It was much the same with us. We had no plan to be swept up by mercy. We were not seeking as He sought us. We are grateful for the change. We do not know many things. But, we are sure on this: We will never again be what we were!

——— TRANSFORMING SAVIOR, ———

We thank You that we are not what we were. Similarly, we are confident that we are not all that we shall be by Your grace.

HARD WORK

For by grace you have been saved through faith, and that not of yourselves; it is the gift of God, not of works, lest anyone should boast.

—Ephesians 2:8, 9

Hard work is a good thing. When we look about and consider our lives, most of us will conclude that we might have done better or risen higher had we worked harder. We must understand biblical truth, however, lest we should expend our labors to no purpose. We ought not attempt to gain salvation by our good works. We are saved by faith in the works of Christ. If we trust in these, we shall never have reason for shame.

——— GRACEFUL SAVIOR, ———

Unregenerate man can have no merit in the eyes of God. There is nothing in our labors that God can accept. Only the work of Christ will suffice. Help us to trust in that alone.

IMAGES

...and changed the glory of the incorruptible God into an image made like corruptible man-- and birds and four-footed animals and creeping things.

—Romans 1:23

Man is a natural idolater. No matter where he is found, he will not be far from a god that he has fashioned with his own hands. He will have a god, but must have one on his own terms. Man's false deities must be reducible to a finite form. He must be subject to control. He must not be quite as just, or nearly so holy. Foolish man! How could we imagine that God is like one of us?

———— IMMUTABLE FATHER, ————

If the whole world were a great temple to Your name, it could never contain You. We praise You that You have condescended to take up residence in us.

FELLOWSHIP

...that I may know Him and the power of
His resurrection, and the fellowship of His
sufferings, being conformed to His death,
—Philemon 3:10

We should be careful what we pray for.
God answered this prayer on behalf
of His beloved apostle. God graced Paul with
prison. He was granted shipwreck. He was
tenderly placed in peril and allowed to go
sleepless and hungry. But, oh, my brothers and
sisters, what sweet fellowship he had! God,
give us a desire to know You in this special and
holy fellowship of Your suffering!

—————— TENDER FATHER, ——————

We are awash in fellowship. We love our
brothers and sisters because You love them.
But, most of all, we love You, Lord. Grant to
us a closer walk.

JOY

Be glad in the Lord and rejoice, you righteous;
and shout for joy, all you upright in heart!
—Psalms 32:11

Our verse is not commending rejoicing and shouts of joy to the unrighteous. If they had a proper grasp of reality, they would be motivated to the deepest groans, and most profound weeping. Joy is for the children of God. It transcends mere circumstance. It is recognition that God loves us and is in control. He will sweep these clouds from the sky. The sun will shine again. Joys will ravish us and they will have no end.

——— FOUNTAIN OF ALL JOY, ———

We are thankful for the joy that we have in You. It is more than thrill or even happiness. It runs deep and flows over. It cannot be contained and it has no end.

LOVE

We love Him because He first loved us.
—1 John 4:19

How consistently the scripture drains us of our pride. We would be puffed up and find superiority in loving God, while others are cold. It is no wonder that we should love the Lord! He is the embodiment of every beauty and grace. But, why should He love Us? We are not told His reasons. He loved us simply because He would. We may never know more than this. But, we shall have an eternity to love Him for it.

——— LOVING SAVIOR, ———

Before grace came to us, our hearts were hard, and could have affection for nothing except worldly things. You have given us a new heart, and we use it to return Your love.

FAITH

"Knowing that a man is not justified by the works of the law but by faith in Jesus Christ..."

—Galatians 2:16

M en are wont to have faith in various things. Many are the times that we have gone to the ballpark with a firm conviction that our team would win. We have maintained a dogged trust in political parties and their candidates, when reason would have dictated otherwise. This misplaced confidence has often led to disappointment and embarrassment. Faith in Jesus Christ will never make us ashamed. It is the rock on which we shall stand in the judgment.

—————— GRACIOUS JUSTIFIER, ——————

We have no holiness with which we might press a claim to Your mercy. It is You that has sought and found us, and has given us faith to believe.

GLORY

And Ezra blessed the Lord, the great God. Then all the people answered, "Amen, Amen!" while lifting up their hands. And they bowed their heads and worshiped the Lord with their faces to the ground.

—Nehemiah 8:6

The glorification of God demands our adoration. It galls us to behold the disrespect shown to God by the current generation. When we behold what actually delights our world, we little wonder that God is not honored. Let every lover of filth be cautioned. The One who is the object of your slights, and insolence will some day be your judge. Let gainsayers put that truth under their pillow tonight, and see if sleep comes!

——— AWESOME SAVIOR, ———

We acknowledge that we are as the dust in the balance when compared to Your greatness. Help us to be humble before You as we ought to be.

JOY

"Most assuredly, I say to you that you will weep and lament, but the world will rejoice; and you will be sorrowful, but your sorrow will be turned into joy."

—John 16:20

Christ here speaks words of encouragement to His disciples. By these words we are taught much. He tells us that when the world is rejoicing, it means tough times for the Christian. We are not to enjoy the same pleasures as those that delight in the world. They would see our Lord crucified. We would see Him glorified. Be encouraged, for Satan's end is near. The Lord's triumph is at hand, and with it, our great and eternal joy.

——— FOUNTAIN OF ALL JOYS, ———
We thank You that our time of joy approaches. The clouds will soon depart, never to be re-gathered, and we will know the unspeakable elation of victory in Christ Jesus.

SUMMER VACATIONS

Before the mountains were brought forth, or ever You had formed the earth and the world, even from everlasting to everlasting, You are God.

—Psalms 90:2

One of the few things that have not changed since I was a child is the fact that the mountains are still where my childhood vacations found them. I am surprised that there has been no governmental project designed to more evenly distribute them. The Lord made them. In the subtlety of the tenses used in our verse, we see that God is independent of time. What a great God is this for whom all of existence is now!

—— O GREAT I AM, ——

Fill us with a sense of Your everlasting being. The mountains were made in time—as were all things including ourselves. But, time itself, is Your creation.

HARVEST TIME

"His Lord said to him, 'Well done, good and faithful servant; you were faithful over a few things, I will make you ruler over many things. Enter into the joy of your Lord.'"

—Matthew 25:21

One man always pastured little churches. They seldom could support him, so he worked the weekdays for wages. On nights and weekends, he strove for the Lord. He will fall to an early frost. Though he labored deep into his season, He will not witness the harvest for which he longed. But, oh, see the joy that awaits! He did not play the fool, but worked while others took their ease. The Lord has noted all, and He is the very great reward.

——— LORD OF THE HARVEST, ———

Help us to see that there is no profit in a life invested in self. Let us take that which we must ultimately surrender, and devote it to that which cannot be taken away.

WAGING THE BATTLE

Stand therefore, having girded your waist with truth, having put on the breastplate of righteousness,

—Ephesians 6:14

It is said that extracting information from captured Japanese soldiers taken prisoner during the early days of Word War II was relatively easy. It seems that they had not been given any instruction as to their behavior if captured. It was just assumed that they would die in battle. Paul goes on in this and subsequent verses to describe the whole armor of God. No protection is provided for the back. It is assumed that there is no retreat.

——— MIGHTY WARRIOR, ———

Mighty forces oppose us. What are they in comparison to Your strength? Give us the courage to engage. Hasten the day when we stand with You upon the field—victorious.

OBEDIENCE

"And all these blessings shall come upon you and overtake you, because you obey the voice of the Lord your God:"

—Deuteronomy 28:2

We are wont to take a wrong view of obedience. Our flesh rebels against this, and would tell our soul that it is an onerous hardship. Think back along the path that has brought you to today. Has obedience to the Lord ever brought you misery and defeat? We must see that blessings come to us as we are in the way of conformance. They will catch us and completely overwhelm us. I am ready to sign-up for some of that!

——— DEAR LORD, ———

We can look back to the blessings that attach to obedience. Cause us to be sensible to that, and to live lives of expectation that there is more to come.

REPENTANCE

Now I rejoice, not that you were made sorry, but that your sorrow led to repentance. For you were made sorry in a godly manner, that you might suffer loss from us in nothing.

—2 Corinthians 7:9

Paul has already written one letter to the Corinthian church. It was a hard letter to write, for it rebuked them. Thank the Lord for His correction. When we feel a sorrow for sin that is of God, remorse is a step toward repentance. A turning from our error brings us the rest of the way. We should know, however, that neither sorrow nor turning is possible for us except by the grace of God.

FORGIVING SAVIOR,

We pray for Your grace. Our flesh will lead us down into the darkness. Help us to crucify our flesh that we may have abundant life in You.

FLEXIBILITY

Then He said to them, "Follow Me, and I will make you fishers of men." They immediately left their nets and followed Him.

—Matthew 4:19, 20

Peter and his brother Andrew were fishermen. Fish were at the hub of their plans for the day. But, Christ was about to change everything without warning. Talk about flexibility! They left the work that was already underway to follow Jesus. Every former plan and aspiration went down the chute! Our hearts must be similarly prepared. These fellows might have finished life with a boat and some nets. Instead, they, by grace, changed the world.

——— HEAVENLY FATHER, ———

Who would have thought that we would come to this place? We were about our own plans when You found us. Continue to direct us so that we do not prematurely fossilize.

HOPE

Hope deferred makes the heart sick, but when the desire comes, it is a tree of life.

—Proverbs 13:12

There have been times in my life when I was almost sick with hope. Would she turn to look at me? Would she consent to be my wife? The more she waited the sicker I became! I have paced the Father's Waiting Room in hopes of a healthy child. I still wait for some of my dreams to be fulfilled. When my hope of heaven is realized, it will be eternally satisfying, like a tree springing up into life eternal.

—— OUR HOPE AND OUR SALVATION, ——

There have been days when hope alone has kept us in the race. Now we near the finish. Our need of hope will dissolve in our first sight of You.

RETIREMENT

"Please let a little water be brought, and wash your feet, and rest yourselves under the tree."
—Genesis 18:4

Like the messengers in our verse, we have come a long way. We are entitled to a little rest. A nap under the trees might be nice, but we are not yet at the end of our journey. We also have urgent business, and we dare not sleep away the opportunity. These men were couriers. In a sense, so are we, and many depend on our message. So take the occasional snooze, but do not devote yourself to ease.

——— FATHER, ———

When the end shall come upon us, let us be found useful. Give us the words to say and the strength and faithfulness to speak them.

IGNORANCE

Now Jericho was securely shut up because of the children of Israel; none went out, and none came in.

—Joshua 6:1

Poor ignorant sinners! How like the people of Jericho they are. They will not let the truth in. Neither will they go out to discover it. Thinking themselves secure behind the ramparts of their own false hopes, they assure one another of their mutual safety. But, stupidity is not an effective substitute for knowledge. Those walls will be breached by the judgment of the Lord. How awful, in that day, when they find out that they were wrong.

——— OMNISCIENT FATHER, ———

We praise You that You did not leave us behind the walls that we had erected against You. You breached them, and carried us away on the wings of Your matchless grace.

SERVANTHOOD

"So likewise you, when you have done all those things which you are commanded, say, 'We are unprofitable servants. We have done what was our duty to do.'"

—Luke 17:10

It is easy for us to exaggerate our merit. We are taught here that we are expected to do all of our duty. Upon completion, we must recognize that we have done no more than we ought. The Lord's service is exacting and His eye is keen for imperfection. We ought to be grateful that He will use our weak efforts at all. He imputes the merit of our Savior to us. It is Christ that makes us acceptable.

——— LOVING MASTER, ———

Heaven is full of angels who do Your bidding swiftly and perfectly. What a great condescension that You should permit our frail and halting efforts on behalf of the Kingdom.

TIES THAT BIND

"A new commandment I give to you, that you love one another; as I have loved you, that you also love one another."

—John 13:34

I am not always a lovely person. Not a few people have confirmed that. I am too quick to judge, to difficult to approach, and slow to demonstrate empathy. Some folks understand me, but that is not the same as real affection. I might despair, except that my family, God's children, and my Lord have found a way to love me. On what basis will I not care for others since God has fixed His love on me?

——— AFFECTIONATE FATHER, ———

I do not wonder how it is that I love You. I have a universe of reasons to do that. What I cannot comprehend is that You have condescended to delight in me.

SUMMER VACATIONS

Those who go down to the sea in ships, who do business on great waters, They see the works of the Lord, and His wonders in the deep.

—Psalms 107:23, 24

One of the huge vacation mistakes that I have made involved a half-day excursion on the ocean in search of whales. We spent a lot of time hung over the railings, although I don't recall searching for wonders in the deep. There is no limit to the wonders of the Lord. He has made all things. We might spend our allocation of days in admiration and never come to the end of our delight.

—— FATHER CREATOR, ——

How marvelous are Your works. We look out and see the heavens. Looking in, we see minute workings of Your fingers. Looking about, we see Your wonderful provision.

TRIUMPH

So it was, when they brought out those kings to Joshua, that Joshua called for all the men of Israel, and said to the captains of the men of war who went with him, "Come near, put your feet on the necks of these kings." And they drew near and put their feet on their necks.

—Joshua 10:24

When the original spies sent by Moses into the Canaan saw these kings, they quaked with fear. Here Joshua calls all Israel to witness their ignominious defeat. By having the men place their feet on the necks of these, he shows them that they ought never to have been afraid. What strength do our enemies possess as compared to those of our Lord? Our lives should reflect our confidence in eventual triumph.

——— LORD OF HOSTS, ———
We thank You for the coming triumph. Let the certainty of it imbue today with confidence and boldness. Replace our natural fears with heavenly boldness.

August

1. Passing It On
2. A Full Quiver
3. Hard Work
4. Ignorance
5. Moving
6. Giving
7. Faith
8. Summer Vacations
9. Ignorance
10. Endings
11. Grief
12. Forgiveness
13. Fellowship
14. Celebration
15. Waging The Battle
16. Hope
17. Love
18. Values
19. Retirement
20. Parting
21. Retirement
22. Simplification
23. Summer Vacations
24. Ties That Bind
25. Forgiveness
26. Triumph
27. Love
28. Servanthood
29. Retirement
30. Heaven
31. Ties That Bind

Passing It On

He first found his own brother Simon, and said to him, "We have found the Messiah" (which is translated, the Christ).

— John 1:41

Andrew had discovered something and he simply could not keep it to himself. This was not news of similar significance to any other thing that he had ever learned. We know how he felt. Messiah is among us! We have met Him, and have spent time with Him. He is real. We do not have to be slaves to sin! He has set us free! Having received this news by grace, we now have the responsibility to pass it on.

Triumphant Lord,

Restore to us the excitement of our first love. How beautiful were the days when we first knew forgiveness. Let the memory of that time spur us to bring this joy to others.

A FULL QUIVER

"O Jerusalem, Jerusalem, the one who kills the prophets and stones those who are sent to her! How often I wanted to gather your children together, as a hen gathers her chicks under her wings, but you were not willing!"

—Matthew 23:37

As Jesus spoke these words, the cup of God's wrath was filling. The Roman legions would soon surround the walls of the ancient city. The temple would be pulled down, and the population slaughtered. As we witness the Lord's love for the children of Jerusalem, let us have a similar heart for our own sons and daughters. While the lamp of mercy still burns, let us strain to gather everyone to the light. Let every little fist knock at the door of God's mercy.

——— FORBEARING LORD, ———

We know that only You can save. We pray that You would consider our children, and extend Your mercy to them. Help us to bear the light of Your truth to them.

Hard Work

Now I beg you, brethren, through the Lord Jesus Christ, and through the love of the Spirit, that you strive together with me in prayers to God for me,

—Romans 15:30

We have many spiritual responsibilities. We must strive to see our spouses safe to heaven. We must see our children within the safety of God's grace. But we must never forget our most sober mission: We must see ourselves in the path of grace all the way to heaven's gates. Let us enlist our Christian brothers and sisters in a mutual compact to work hard in prayer for one another. Then will our enemies fall and glory be magnified.

— Perfect Provider, —

The night is long and our souls are yet far from home. Show us the light of Your grace that it may draw us into that safe haven of Your mercy.

IGNORANCE

"So he said, 'I will do this: I will pull down my barns and build greater, and there I will store all my crops and my goods.'"

—Luke 12:18

We are an ignorant race. We have it in our minds that we will live forever. We drive our roots deep, and lay up great treasure for the future. We have no thought for the hereafter. We build new barns but another will hoard treasure there. We store much food but someone else will eat it. Lord, give us the sense to see that we are but fragile flowers who are here today and vanished for eternity.

——— OMNISCIENT FATHER, ———

Help us to build upon eternal foundations. When the judgment comes, hide us away in the Rock of Ages.

MOVING

Then Joseph took an oath from the children of Israel, saying, "God will surely visit you, and you shall carry up my bones from here."
—Genesis 50:25

Joseph was a "big shooter" in the land of Egypt. The bad news is that he would much rather have been elsewhere. He was an heir to the promise. He would know a better land. Here, he makes his brethren swear that they will move him from this place. We have a similar promise from the Lord Jesus. He will not leave our bodies in this land. He will speak and our bones will rise to incorruption and glory.

——— HEAVENLY FATHER, ———

Prepare our hearts for our moving day. Detach us from the affections that we hold for this present world. Direct our hearts toward heaven.

GIVING

But the manifestation of the Spirit is given to each one for the profit of all:

—1 Corinthians 12:7

How wonderful is God that He is the source of every gift? Whatever talents or skills we have, it is very plain from our verse that they are from God. Further, they are not bestowed upon us to be squandered. They are for our brothers and sisters in Christ. Not just for their enjoyment, but for their profit. Let the generosity of our Father be proclaimed through the rich gifts that He has bestowed on His children!

—— GIVING LORD, ——

What do we have that You have not given to us? Let us make it our work to use Your gifts for Your glory.

FAITH

"I have been crucified with Christ; it is no longer I who live, but Christ lives in me; and the life which I now live in the flesh I live by faith in the Son of God, who loved me and gave Himself for me."

—Galatians 2:20

The future for the old man was not bright. He was immersed in sin and antagonistic toward God. He is dead now. He got what he deserved upon Christ's cross. A new life has come on the wings of faith. Since we died in Him, we are also raised with Him. We live now to serve the Lord. The old man is a memory. The new is an eternal monument to the grace of God through faith.

—————— LOVING SAVIOR, ——————

Our faith is dear, but we would be parted from it. It is ours to enjoy those things, which we cannot now see. Hasten the day when our faith will be dissolved in sight.

SUMMER VACATIONS

"And many nations will pass by this city; and everyone will say to his neighbor, 'Why has the Lord done so to this great city?'"

—Jeremiah 22:8

My wife and I like to vacation in a different metropolis each year to do our Christmas shopping. It seems to take a bit of the work out of it. Cities simultaneously attract and repel. They are wonderful concentrations of culture and talent, and yet are also great magnets for the attraction of evil. When we see the kind of open sin that is common today, we know that the judgment of God is not far behind.

——— MERCIFUL FATHER, ———

We praise You for Your forbearance. We know that You might justly bring down our great buildings and pull up the monuments of our rebellion. Grant us repentance and faith.

IGNORANCE

The twelve gates were twelve pearls: each individual gate was of one pearl. And the street of the city was pure gold, like transparent glass.

—Revelation 21:21

Pity the Christian who works only for wages that are paid out in the coin of this temporal realm. He scrapes and scampers for worldly gains. He sets no importance on the accumulation of heavenly treasure. Every thought is devoted and every movement calculated to bring an increase of gold. Imagine the disbelief of our heavenly friends when he is left to explain that he spent his entire life in the accumulation of street pavement.

——— OMNISCIENT FATHER, ———

Help us to know what is truly valuable. We are carried off by silly desires to gain things that are fleeting. Anchor us in You wisdom so that we dare not stray.

ENDINGS

Therefore, if anyone is in Christ, he is a new creation; old things have passed away; behold, all things have become new.

—2 Corinthians 5:17

At our age, we might mistake the meaning of "old things" in this verse. What is here referenced is our old manner of living. Our old world-view, affections, pleasure, friends, and expectations have been erased by the brightness of Christ's appearing in our lives. We surrender all of these things and more, that we might have a portion in Jesus. The exchange has been greatly to our advantage. It is all undeserved! It is all grace!

——— GRACIOUS LORD, ———

We thank You that You have put an end to our old desires, and fancies. You have also implanted within us a yearning for what we shall be. Lord, hasten the day.

GRIEF

So Peter went out and wept bitterly.
—Luke 22:62

Peter has failed his Master and Friend. We have all tasted this grief. We would have been more brave, more righteous, more faithful, more kind, more constant, or more gracious. The misery of moral shortfall is common to mankind. Be of good cheer, however, because Christ died for these sins, also. Moreover, a day is coming when He will wipe all the tears from our eyes. Sinless, and immortal—we shall never know regret again.

— FORGIVING LORD, —

We have failed You often, and we make no excuse for it. The good news is that Christ is our all-sufficient Savior whose blood covers these griefs also.

FORGIVENESS

Finally, there is laid up for me the crown of righteousness, which the Lord, the righteous Judge, will give to me on that Day, and not to me only but also to all who have loved His appearing.

—2 Timothy 4:8

Many of us have done awful things. Memory of them causes us to be unable to rise above the past, and to feel good about ourselves. We need to understand that we are forgiven of God. Not only so, but we have the righteousness of Christ imputed to us. While there may not have been anyone worse than us in the past, there is now no one better either. Salvation is a great leveler in this way.

——— FORGIVING LORD, ———

You have done so much for us. You have lifted us up and made of us a royal priesthood. You have set us in high places. All of this was done for us. Therefore, make us humble.

FELLOWSHIP

Rejoice with those who rejoice, and weep with those who weep.

—ROMANS 12:15

We might wish that our fellowship had only to do with rejoicing. No doubt, it is a rich and wonderful experience to celebrate the blessings of God when they bedew the lips with laughter and song. But, life also winds through paths of sorrow. What a great privilege to come beside that brother or sister in Christ with a comforting word as they drink deeply of sufferings. Only Christ and Christian friends shine light into these dark places.

——— HOLY COMFORT, ———

We are brought into difficult places. Sometimes the troubles are so thick about us that they block the sun. Please stay near us, and give us a sense of Your presence.

CELEBRATION

They shall utter the memory of Your great goodness, and shall sing of Your righteousness.

—Psalms 145:7

A t this age, much of our treasure is memory. What does this generation know of kerosene lamps, streetcars, five-cent pay phones, hitch-hiking, disciplined school-rooms, or hula hoops? These are dear remembrances, but they are attached to that which is in itself fleeting. Do you recollect when grace came to you? Can you recall the thrill of God's deliverance? Reflect on gracious answers to fervent prayer. God has been good. These things are cause for celebration.

—— BENEVOLENT FATHER, ——

If we received the world that we deserve, it would be full of darkness, and evil. We thank You for Your grace which has given us beauty and good.

WAGING THE BATTLE

"And the Lord your God will drive out those nations before you little by little..."
—Deuteronomy 7:22

Here is a precious promise. God will go before us and He will defeat our spiritual enemies for us. Before you head for the beach, expecting to follow the news of battle in the daily newspapers—note the little words "before you" The Lord will go "before" us, but He will not go "for" us. Victory cannot be achieved from the couch. We must personally enter the fray. If we do that, God will achieve the victory.

——— VICTORIOUS FATHER, ———

We are lethargic. We are wont to laze away the day while others bleed and die. You have waged the war before us. Give us the faith to follow You to victory.

HOPE

"Blessed is the man who trusts in the Lord, and whose hope is the Lord."

—Jeremiah 17:7

Perhaps we have children or grandchildren who are far from the Lord. It may be that they are immersed in sins that bind and blight. They live lives as though they were black holes from which no particle escapes. Not even a ray of light emerges. In these situations, we are blessed if we trust the Lord. He opens all doors, and bends the strongest will. He is our only hope. There is nothing too hard for Him.

—— OUR HOPE AND OUR SALVATION, ——
We are glad that You are our God. There is nothing too difficult for You. Cause the locked places to be opened. Make the light shine into the darkness.

LOVE

"For God so loved the world that He gave His only begotten Son, that whoever believes in Him should not perish but have everlasting life."

—John 3:16

We live in a strange world where love has been diminished to a process of taking. A scriptural love always involves giving. Our heavenly Father is the example for us. He loved us simply because He would. We were in a terrible state of loss and there was no hope for us unless He should give a great gift to us. Jesus is that gift. Should we reject Him, then we have no hope and will certainly perish.

—— LOVING SAVIOR, ——

We thank You for Your sacrificial love toward us. How precious is the Gift that seals Your love to us!

VALUES

... the murderer shall surely be put to death.
—Numbers 35:16

Missing from contemporary society is the value of fairness. In taking a life, the murderer steals all that a person has or ever will have in this world. He strikes at the image and law of His creator. If we are concerned for the perpetrator, we have little thought for God, or for victims. I might lie awake all night in anger over injustice. But I know that the Lord has noted every deed. Vengeance is His. He will repay.

——— JUST LORD, ———

We can expect no justice in our courts. But this should not persuade us that wrong is not always avenged. We praise You that You will make every crooked place strait.

RETIREMENT

"But whoever listens to me will dwell safely, and will be secure, without fear of evil."
— Proverbs 1:33

Retirement is all about security. We would desire to have a little money in the bank. A good pension would be nice. It would be a blessing if the government would keeps its hands out of our pockets. Quiet and safe neighborhoods are a plus. Still, there is no safety if the Lord does not protect us. If we have heeded His call to repentance and seek to obey His law, He will build a protective fence around us.

GREAT PROTECTOR,

The night is dark and we are still far from home. Evil forces pursue us, and all of Your enemies are ours. If You will be our security, we cannot be harmed.

PARTING

So Sarah died in Kirjath Arba (that is, Hebron) in the land of Canaan, and Abraham came to mourn for Sarah and to weep for her.
—Genesis 23:2

The history of our race is a history of tears. The great patriarch was not exempted from grief. Sarah was his fair flower. She was a sharer in great promises. Both knew the pain of separation from home and people. They were together in a life-long pilgrimage. Neither had ever owned an acre in the land that God had given them. They part here in this life, but God has foreordained a rich and glorious reunion.

——— KINDLY LORD, ———

We are a dull and uncomprehending people. Give us the faith to appropriate these great truths that bring reality and reason to these difficult times.

RETIREMENT

And He said, "My Presence will go with you, and I will give you rest."

—Exodus 33:14

Many of us are retired. Others are, at least, thinking about it. Maybe the desire grows strong to curl up with a nice book, or a good crossword puzzle and idle away the time. Our verse would instruct, however, that there is no basis for rest unless He is with us. It is madness to laze away the hours if God's judgment threatens. We must make sure that we have things in their proper order.

—— FATHER, ——

Help us to hear Your knock upon the door of our hearts. Give us the grace to open ourselves to You, and know the peace and rest that comes with Your presence.

SIMPLIFICATION

Then Abram moved his tent, and went and dwelt by the terebinth trees of Mamre, which are in Hebron, and built an altar there to the Lord.

—Genesis 13:18

It is a matter of some irony that Abram lives in tents while others enjoy fine houses that are built on his land. Perhaps God kept his life simple so that he would not be distracted by a proliferation of things. If the Lord called Abram to move, all he had to do was fold the tent, load the camels, and get on down the road. Do we presume on God when we cumber ourselves with so much stuff?

—— DEAR LORD, ——

Help us to see that is world is neither our treasure, nor our permanent home. We are pilgrims here. Help us not to trust in things, but to put our confidence in You alone.

SUMMER VACATIONS

You will show me the path of life; in Your presence is fullness of joy; at Your right hand are pleasures forevermore.

—Psalms 16:11

I remember taking the family on vacation to a major theme park when admittance involved a booklet of tickets to the various attractions. Nowhere on earth could the imagination and excitement be matched! Still, if these rare novelties became every day things, the enjoyment would eventually pale and the excitement fizzle. It is not so with the Lord. He is infinite. Every occasion in His presence imbues us with new delights. Each encounter brings joys never before known.

FATHER OF LIGHTS,

You are ever new, yet we know that there are pleasures that we cannot yet experience. Hasten the day when, as immortal and holy persons, we may fully enjoy You forever.

TIES THAT BIND

Jesus answered and said to him, "Most assuredly, I say to you, unless one is born again, he cannot see the kingdom of God."

—John 3:3

I remember tying a bath towel around my neck and leaping off the garage roof. My comic book heroes were not earth-bound, and I did not want to be either. The natural man or woman is bound by the gravity of sin. They cannot soar on spiritual wings. Sin weighs them down. Unless grace should relieve the burden, they will never rise to see the Kingdom, nor will they ever care to know its King.

——— DEAR GIVER OF LIFE, ———

Lord, we thank You for Your goodness and grace. Lift our load of sin, and open our eyes to the beauty of righteousness and the wonders of Your Kingdom.

FORGIVENESS

...and delivered righteous Lot, who was oppressed by the filthy conduct of the wicked...

—2 Peter 2:7

This is a hopeful and instructive verse. Poor Lot's pilgrimage was very much a failure. Not only did he ruin himself, but also, every life that was dependent on his. His wife was dead, his daughters disgraced, his fortune gone, and his descendants a scourge to Israel for millennia. There was much to charge against his account. Yet, he is here called "righteous." That is the kind of forgiveness I need, and have through Christ Jesus.

——— FORGIVING FATHER, ———

We learn of Lot, and we are encouraged by our knowledge. We are not successful in all that we undertake. Hold us close so that we do not disgrace Your love for us.

TRIUMPH

Therefore David ran and stood over the Philistine, took his sword and drew it out of its sheath and killed him, and cut off his head with it. And when the Philistines saw that their champion was dead, they fled.

—1 Samuel 17:51

Talk about bad days! Poor Goliath filled the air with bragging and threats. His swagger must have worn a path between the opposing armies. Now, a mere boy has defeated him, he has completely lost his head, and his remains are being exhibited to all his old friends. From David's side, it appears to be all triumph. He did not put his trust in armament or weapons. Victory came by grace, and the glory was the Lord's.

——— GOD OF OUR FATHERS, ———

We look forward to the day of Your triumph. That will not be limited and local, as was David's. It will be universal, complete, and final. Hide us then in Your grace.

LOVE

... having loved His own who were in the world, He loved them to the end.

—John 13:1

We are not much at living up to our commitments in our day. We tend to jettison obligations when they become inconvenient. Babies are not allowed to come to term if their birth will cause hardship. It is better to bankrupt than to honor our financial promises. Marriages are ended when they require work or fidelity. It was not so with our Lord. He was faithful to His own until the end, and so ought we to be.

—— LOVING SAVIOR, ——

Let us be constant in our love. Cause us not to waver in our fidelity to You. We are weak and prone to stray. Hold us close until we are safe at home with You.

SERVANTHOOD

Let a man so consider us, as servants of Christ and stewards of the mysteries of God.
—1 Corinthians 4:1

Not long after a personal introduction, we find that we cannot forbear to ask, "What do you do?" How many times have you replied, "I am a servant of Jesus Christ"? It is noble work, and it bespeaks certain humility. We go at the Lord's bidding. We are not fountains of original thought. We are authorized only to speak what we are commanded. But, we are entrusted with deep mysteries, and we are commanded to share them.

——— MASTER, ———

We are thankful for the divine wisdom with which we are entrusted. Help us to be bold in proclaiming Your truth to others.

Retirement

So Jonah went out of the city and sat on the east side of the city. There he made himself a shelter and sat under it in the shade, till he might see what would become of the city.

—Jonah 4:5

One might say that Jonah had been a mite reluctant. He did not want God to show mercy to Nineveh. But, God had been pretty persistent, and finally prevailed on Jonah to preach to those folks. Now our friend has retired to the edge of town where he sits in the shade waiting to see what will happen. Jonah is like some of us. He would rather die than to see God's mercy poured out on his enemies.

—— Lord, ——

Fix our evil hearts. Help us to see the great mercies that You have extended to us. Help us to see that Your love knows no boundary or race.

HEAVEN

But as it is written: "Eye has not seen, nor ear heard, nor have entered into the heart of man the things which God has prepared for those who love Him."

—1 Corinthians 2:9

It's hard, in many ways, to talk about heaven. Not because we don't want to, or don't believe in it, but because we simply do not have the words. If we nudge our minds to imagine the most beautiful, glorious, perfect, eternal place that we can, we still do not enter its sacred precincts. It will all be new. The unfamiliarity of it would be daunting except that Jesus is there. We know Him, and He will make it home!

——— HEAVENLY FATHER, ———

There is a restlessness in us now. It is almost as though we hear the rustle of angels' wings. Sharpen our spiritual senses so that we may ready ourselves for heavenly things.

TIES THAT BIND

Now when he had finished speaking to Saul, the soul of Jonathan was knit to the soul of David, and Jonathan loved him as his own soul.

—1 Samuel 18:1

It is good to have chums. In my old neighborhood, having a buddy meant that anyone wanting to fight me would have to fight him also. A fellow could not have too many friends. Many people come to the end of their lives without one single intimate acquaintance. Though I am unworthy of so fine a relationship, nevertheless, Christ has condescended to call me friend. If you pick on me, you have to answer to Him.

——— MIGHTY DEFENDER, ———

Thank You for Your care of us. How often have we desired to flee to safety under Your wings? You have loved our souls, and You shelter them there against the night.

September

1. Grief
2. Simplification
3. Holiness
4. Homecoming
5. Retirement
6. Repentance
7. Parting
8. Clutter
9. Experience
10. Moving
11. Gleaning
12. Crowns
13. Passing It On
14. Giving
15. Hard Work
16. Obedience
17. Changes
18. Images
19. Holiness
20. Beginnings
21. Glory
22. Faith
23. Hard Work
24. Harvest Time
25. Fall Colors
26. Flexibility
27. Retirement
28. Fellowship
29. Hope
30. Harvest Time

GRIEF

So David arose from the ground, washed and anointed himself, and changed his clothes; and he went into the house of the Lord and worshiped. Then he went to his own house; and when he requested, they set food before him, and he ate.

—2 Samuel 12:20

We all know of those who have spent large portions of their lives in mourning for the dead. Certainly it is right and good that we should grieve, but not overmuch. We all bear wounds of loss that never heal in this life. Prolonged public grieving ignores the precious promises that we hold concerning those who "sleep" in Christ. In light of these, it is proper that we cease sorrowing, and don the glad face of expectation.

——— UNDERSTANDING LORD, ———
We are at an age when the reapers scythe harvests all about us. Our hearts are broken when we count the loss. Give us a right view so that we do not grieve overmuch.

SIMPLIFICATION

So Joshua answered them, "If you are a great people, then go up to the forest country and clear a place for yourself there in the land of the Perizzites and the giants, since the mountains of Ephraim are too confined for you."

—Joshua 17:15

The tribes of Ephraim and Manasseh have a problem to which we can relate. They need more space, or so they are convinced. They have title to land, but have insufficient courage to take all that God has given them. Similarly, we desire to grow spiritually, but feel constrained by the strength of our imagined foes. We need to simplify our approach. God has given us all we need. We must, by faith, seize what He has given.

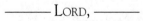

——— LORD, ———

We are impoverished amid plenty. We are blinded so that we are unable to see what sits on the shelf. Give us light to see Your bounty, and faith to appropriate it.

HOLINESS

"He who is unjust, let him be unjust still; he who is filthy, let him be filthy still; he who is righteous, let him be righteous still; he who is holy, let him be holy still."

—Revelation 22:11

Remember when it was your delight to make childish faces? Recall your mother warning, "What if your face should freeze in that position?" Something like that will occur in the spiritual world someday. There are many who presume upon God's goodness. They will repent sometime. Suddenly, judgment falls and they are consigned to be forever what they are—filthy. Thank God today for the holiness of Christ imputed to you.

——— HOLY FATHER, ———

Lift us from the vileness wherein You found us. Give us a thirst for righteousness that cannot be slaked. Cause us to strive toward Your holy standard.

HOMECOMING

And devout men carried Stephen to his burial, and made great lamentation over him.

—Acts 8:2

I want to be missed when I die. I have an admiration for Stephen. Not only was he a good man, and bold in the Lord, but there were many who loved him. Being mindful of our own funeral procession might cause us all to be nicer people. More important than my send-off, in my mind, is my homecoming reception at the other end. I know that Christ will have prepared everything for my arrival.

HEAVENLY FATHER,

We are gathered one by one into the Father's house. There will come a day when the last of God's elect will hear the gospel call. Then we shall all be safe at home.

RETIREMENT

Then Gideon went up by the road of those who dwell in tents on the east of Nobah and Jogbehah; and he attacked the army while the camp felt secure.

—Judges 8:11

Gideon's quarry has been on the run. They have been in flight for about a day, and cannot imagine that any foe would have the fortitude to continue pursuit. While they rest, judgment will fall on them. We have been long in the battle. The enemy might expect that we would retire and he might have nothing more to fear from us. By the grace of God, let's be a big surprise to him by pressing the battle.

———— HEAVENLY FATHER, ————

The bloom of youth has faded from us, but our eye is still keen for Your glory. Grant us grace to continue our fight until You grant the victory.

REPENTANCE

Then Zacchaeus stood and said to the Lord, "Look, Lord, I give half of my goods to the poor; and if I have taken anything from anyone by false accusation, I restore fourfold."
—Luke 19:8

Here is a case of genuine repentance! Zacchaeus has had his hand in the cookie jar. He has extorted money from honest people. So profound is his sorrow for his misdeeds that he will not be satisfied until he has made things right with the people that he has cheated. A straight compensation is not enough to assuage the conscience of this little man. He will restore fourfold. It is a small thing as compared to what he has gained.

———— FORGIVING SAVIOR, ————

Give us a heart of repentance. Let the joy of sins forgiven drive our actions. Cause us to make things right with those whom we have offended.

PARTING

"But now he is dead; why should I fast? Can I bring him back again? I shall go to him, but he shall not return to me."

—2 Samuel 12:23

The child is dead. It is an ending. Though he was ever so innocent, he has breathed his last, and there is no remedy for it. Death is final: A threshold crossed from which there is no returning. We are parted and are not to be joined again in this world. This is not all, however, as Christ has purchased a reunion for us. He has removed the sting from death, and someday will put an end to death itself.

——— KINDLY LORD, ———

Death is a consistent thread that runs throughout our history. How precious then is the promise that You will put an end to it.

CLUTTER

"When I saw among the spoils a beautiful Babylonian garment, two hundred shekels of silver, and a wedge of gold weighing fifty shekels, I coveted them and took them. And there they are, hidden in the earth in the midst of my tent, with the silver under it."

—Joshua 7:21

Poor Achan! He has placed an appetite for things above his desire for obedience. After he obtained them he had to bury them. What satisfaction were they to him, buried under the floor of his tent? They were clutter! Have we stolen from God? Let us search our hearts and homes. I pray we find nothing there that would come between our Father and ourselves.

—— BOUNTIFUL FATHER, ——

We have nothing except that which You have given to us. What one among us can say that he has made a debtor of God? We praise You for Your goodness.

Experience

"And if it seems evil to you to serve the Lord, choose for yourselves this day whom you will serve, ... But as for me and my house, we will serve the Lord."

—Joshua 24:15

We are now a bit long in the tooth. Many are the opportunities that have passed us by. Better that we had made other choices. Clearly, some of options are gone forever. There would have been advantage to have cast our lot with God in our youth. How much pain might we have avoided had we done that? Still, that's water under the bridge. Looking forward, what better time to seek His forgiveness and guidance than this moment?

—— Patient Redeemer, ——

You have waited long for us to hear Your voice. How tenderly it speaks of love and forgiveness. Let today be the day of our hearing.

SEPTEMBER 10

MOVING

And Enoch walked with God; and he was not, for God took him.

—Genesis 5:24

Enoch is a nearly unique character in scripture. He is the object of a very special moving day. I hope that it may also be said of us that we walk with God. If so, then we may expect that we too will be relocated some day. Let us be so much like him that we disappear entirely, and all that may be seen, even by those who look ever so closely, is the Lord.

———— HEAVENLY FATHER, ————

Let us be like Enoch. Cause our lives to be so holy that the world will not be worthy of us. Let us have a closer walk with You.

GLEANING

So she gleaned in the field until evening, and beat out what she had gleaned, and it was about an ephah of barley.

—Ruth 2:17

Sometimes there is much work involved if our souls are to be fed. Often spiritual food must be pursued late into the evening. We die of ignorance if we wait for another to feed us. We must discipline our minds to beat upon the Word late into the night. In this way, the chaff of our fleshly understanding may be separated from the purity of God's truth. He does not fail to reward those who diligently seek Him.

—— TEACHER AND FRIEND, ——

We thank You for Your word and Your Spirit, which feed our souls. Give us the desire to seek after You with diligence so that we may truly know You.

CROWNS

His eyes were like a flame of fire, and on His head were many crowns. He had a name written that no one knew except Himself.

—Revelation 19:12

I get excited about the crowns that I will wear some day. I realize that I am only an object of grace. But, this is not so of our Redeemer. He is worthy! Once He wore a crown of thorns for me. Behold Him now, through the eyes of John. He wears a garment dipped in blood, upon a white horse, with eyes that penetrate and burn. Hide me in that day, O Rock of Ages.

——— RIGHTEOUS JUDGE, ———

Our ears burn with disgust as we hear Your name reviled. How good it is to know that You have a name that no other knows. It is pure and untarnished by this world.

PASSING IT ON

Moreover, brethren, I declare to you the gospel which I preached to you, which also you received and in which you stand,
—1 Corinthians 15:1

It is a sad thing in our day, that even among Christians, we have contempt for the preaching of the gospel. The unregenerate mind will hear it and declare it to be foolishness. It does not have the flash and dazzle of theater or fireworks. All that can be said for it is that God has commanded it. By means of this weak tool, the nations of the world have been blessed. Pass it on!

—— TRIUMPHANT LORD, ——

Help us to love the preaching of Your Word. By the weak things of this world, You have chosen to confound the strong. Cause us to preach the Word until You come.

GIVING

Pursue love, and desire spiritual gifts ...
—1 Corinthians 14:1

Here is a good test of our spirituality. If we were to poll our brothers and sisters as to what gifts they might desire from the Father, what do we expect that they would reply? To the extent that we desire first earthly things, we err greatly. It is not that these things have no importance; it is that they are passing. Spiritual gifts are eternal for they profit His church. Only the spiritual yields treasure in heaven.

——— GIVING LORD, ———

We thank You for eternal treasure. Keep our eyes upon it. Deflect us from a desire for that which will only fade and pass away.

HARD WORK

'But the Egyptians mistreated us, afflicted us, and laid hard bondage on us.'
—Deuteronomy 26:6

God has given me a comfortable home, which is mostly empty now of little voices, and the daily riot of children and grandchildren. In the quiet, my thoughts are brought to dwell on the goodness of God. How mightily was I required to labor under my former master! My fellows in the old way struggle still to earn the rest that comes to me by grace. I will pause a while and meditate on this.

——— GRACEFUL SAVIOR, ———

It is all grace. Empty our thoughts of a merited salvation. Our works are filthy rags to You. Only the work done for us by Jesus can satisfy our debt.

OBEDIENCE

"However, if you do not obey the voice of the Lord, but rebel against the commandment of the Lord, then the hand of the Lord will be against you, as it was against your fathers."

—1 Samuel 12:15

We are a stupid lot! It is as though we cannot learn from our past. We delude ourselves that we can fly under the radar of God's wrath. It does not seem to matter that this has always been a tragic course for us. We are blind to the fact that disobedience has brought ruin to our fathers. Lord, hasten the day when we shall be free of our present foolishness, and at liberty to perfectly serve You.

——— DEAR LORD, ———

We live in the promise of a new body. Help us to yearn for that wonderful day when we will be fitted to perfectly serve You. Until then let us press toward Your holiness.

CHANGES

And having been set free from sin, you became slaves of righteousness.

—Romans 6:18

The scripture teaches that we are never entirely at liberty. Freedom is an illusion. Sin had captured our hearts. It had gained the reins of our will. Satan, who could not love us, delighted in our self-destruction. Oh blessed change! Grace apprehended us and immediately took control of our will. We began to love righteousness. Our souls desired to be under His law. Now we have no greater pleasure than to serve Him. Let it ever be so!

——— CHANGELESS LORD, ———

In our relationship with You we have known much alteration. We praise You that the change has not been in You, but in us as we conform ourselves to Your glorious image.

IMAGES

For whom He foreknew, He also predestined to be conformed to the image of His Son, that He might be the firstborn among many brethren.

—Romans 8:29

Unrepentant man is forever making images. He would care to make a god for himself that is to his own liking. The regenerate man is also about the business of fashioning. The Christian would care to remake himself. He would pare away the imperfections eliminating the selfishness, bitterness, self-will, hatred, evil desires, and greed. He would remake himself, by grace, into the image of Christ. We shall know that we are at last truly saved when we are like Him.

——— IMMUTABLE FATHER, ———

Help us to begin today to chip away, removing every little feature that does not conform to Your wonderful image. Hasten the day when we will be like You.

HOLINESS

...because it is written, "Be holy, for I am holy."

—1 Peter 1:16

Our lives are a collection of worn and faded yesterdays. We may lose ourselves in grieving that they were not more useful to ourselves, and to the Kingdom of God. But, they are gone, and we cannot call them again. It would have been good had we been holy then, but there is no better time for holiness than now! Thank the Father that He has granted this time for repentance. Be holy for God is holy!

——— HOLY FATHER, ———

We are not satisfied with ourselves. There is still so much about us that is unworthy. Help us to be holy.

BEGINNINGS

"Then the Lord said to me, 'Arise, begin your journey before the people, that they may go in and possess the land which I swore to their fathers to give them.'"

—Deuteronomy 10:11

Holiness should be the product of a long life spent following the Master. According to our verse, we do this not only for ourselves, but also for those who would follow us. The bright eyes of children and grandchildren should behold our careful walk. We should seek to fully enjoy our spiritual estate. Let them see our energy for the things of Christ as we endeavor to possess all that Christ's blood purchased for us.

——— UNDERSTANDING FATHER, ———

Help us to see that we do not live without influencing others. Let that influence be for the advancement of Your Kingdom and the glory of Your grace.

GLORY

"You shall love the Lord your God with all your heart, with all your soul, and with all your strength."

—Deuteronomy 6:5

We cannot glorify God if we do not love Him. Though the unredeemed person is at enmity with his Creator, this does not diminish the preposterousness of not adoring Him. There is not one single good in the entire inventory of our existence that does not come freely from His hand. Our Christian ardor is multiplied as our hearts are filled with the realization that if we love Him at all, it is because He first loved us.

——— LOVING LORD, ———

The fall brought upon us a spiritual death from which we could neither see, nor desire Your glory. Out of our new spiritual life, we praise You and ardently adore You.

FAITH

That the genuineness of your faith, being much more precious than gold that perishes, though it is tested by fire, may be found to praise, honor, and glory at the revelation of Jesus Christ,

—1 Peter 1:7

Gold and silver are the trivial tokens of worldly wealth. We value them too much. It is God who has real worth. Let us have an interest in Him by faith. Hard times will come. Storms of tribulation may pass over us. Winds of trial may sweep the shiny baubles of earthly delights away, but real faith abides. It has eternal substance. We will cling to it until it be exchanged for sight at the revelation of Christ.

——— OUR HEAVENLY TREASURE, ———

We have brought nothing into this world, and we pity the one who takes nothing out. Worldly things are left behind, but our treasure in You increases.

HARD WORK

"In the sweat of your face you shall eat bread till you return to the ground, for out of it you were taken; for dust you are, and to dust you shall return."

—Genesis 3:19

Sometimes I find it hard to love father Adam. He certainly brought a lot of pain to himself and our mother Eve. Since there is more than enough work to go around, I find myself toweling my old bald head aplenty on a summer's day. We will have work to do in heaven, but not of this sort. With body and heart made new and perfect for service, the effort and drudgery will be gone. There are no weeds in heaven's garden.

——— PATIENT PROVIDER, ———

We have worked many a long day under the bright sun of Your wrath. Thank You for bringing us under the shelter of Your Love.

Harvest Time

For he who sows to his flesh will of the flesh reap corruption, but he who sows to the Spirit will of the Spirit reap everlasting life.

—Galatians 6:8

We are told that all roads lead to God and Glory. Idler and laborer both eat at the end of the day. Many a head will sleep in peace tonight caressing this error. God is not fooled. He cannot be made to love our sin—nor honor it either! Don't be deluded by those who will whisper a false peace to your soul. At harvest time, it will make a difference what we planted.

——— Lord of the Harvest, ———

Waken our senses to the error that exalts the efforts of men. The only work that You will accept is that which was performed on our behalf by the Lord Jesus.

FALL COLORS

And he blessed Joseph, and said: "God, before whom my fathers Abraham and Isaac walked, the God who has fed me all my life long to this day,

—Genesis 48:15

Jacob is now an old man. Our verse finds him in the late autumn of his days. Looking back over the bright colors of his journey, the old man's heart is full of thanksgiving, and he blesses God. We must confess with Jacob that the Lord has laden our tables with many choice and rich meats. We were ever needy, and never deserving, yet His goodness to us did not fail. Have we another friend so kind?

—— KINDLY PROVIDER, ——

Though our eye may dim with age, still the colors of Your goodness remain vibrant in our memory. Your faithfulness warms our expectation for tomorrow.

FLEXIBILITY

Not that I speak in regard to need, for I have
learned in whatever state I am, to be content:
—Philemon 4:11

Many of us could testify to half of what
Paul states here. We have good times
and bad. It is in this matter of contentment
that our experience diverges from that of the
apostle. Paul has a lot of flexibility. If this life
is all, then it is important that we spend it in
plenty and ease. But a blissful eternity awaits
the Christian—therefore, what difference
does it make if we are a little short of comfort
today?

—— WONDERFUL SAVIOR, ——

You left the center of heaven's glory to become
like us. That condescension merits our pause
and consideration. Help us to be like You,
whether it be in poverty, or riches.

RETIREMENT

Then Abram said, "Look, You have given me no offspring; indeed one born in my house is my heir!"

— Genesis 15:3

Pity the poor patriarch. He is a rich man, and yet he has no heirs. At retirement, the estate planners descend upon us. Some of us are wont to ask, "What is the point of a trust if there are no sons and daughters?" If we have no physical progeny, we must not forget that we may indeed use our resources to plant and water gospel seed for the next generation. By this means, we may beget heavenly children.

——— FATHER OF OUR REST, ———
Help us to be responsible with the wealth that You have entrusted to us. Give us a concern for those that come after us.

FELLOWSHIP

Therefore let us pursue the things which make for peace and the things by which one may edify another.

—Romans 14:19

It is appropriate and expected that with the passage of years, we ought to equip ourselves with weapons to deploy against the devil. But, I find myself some mornings with a biblical knife all honed to skewer a brother or sister that I have judged to be in error. Occasionally a big-game hunter has also pursued me. God forbid that I should ever do that again—or have it done to me! Lord, teach me the fellowship of peace!

——— PRINCE OF PEACE, ———

We are a fractious people. It is our flesh that ignites in passion against our brothers and sisters. Help us to be controlled by Your Spirit. Give us brotherly love and peace.

HOPE

Do not be a terror to me; you are my hope in the day of doom.

—Jeremiah 17:17

Doom approaches. Many neither believe that, nor have fears related to it. The scripture says that they are fools! God causes the hearts of some to fear that He might relieve those fears in the person of Christ. It is in the promise of the Lord that the Christian hopes. God cannot fail, and He cannot lie. Therein is our hope.

—— OUR HOPE AND OUR SALVATION, ——
You are our fortress and our high tower. We have no enemy that can stand against You. Be our comfort now as the day draws to a close.

HARVEST TIME

So Joseph died, being one hundred and ten years old; and they embalmed him, and he was put in a coffin in Egypt.

—Genesis 50:26

We have lived long—sometimes in places we didn't care much for. We have worked for people that we didn't like, and have done things that galled. By grace, we were allowed to see beyond this place, and we don't want to be left here in the harvest. Joseph died in the promise that they would remove his bones from Egypt. Similarly, they may plant us where we fall, but by grace will live eternally in the presence of Christ.

——— LORD OF THE HARVEST, ———

For most of us, this has been a rich life, and we thank You for it. But, You have tuned our hearts to better things. Hasten the day when we shall see, and rest in You.

October

1. Harvest Time
2. Brothers and Sisters
3. Fall Colors
4. Flexibility
5. Fall Colors
6. Grief
7. Harvest Time
8. Endings
9. Forgiveness
10. Giving
11. Harvest Time
12. Fall Colors
13. Heaven
14. Holiness
15. Relationships
16. Experience
17. Harvest Time
18. Joy
19. Fall Colors
20. Pasing It On
21. Triumph
22. Gleaning
23. Moving
24. Relationships
25. Simplification
26. Values
27. Fall Colors
28. Waging the Battle
29. Sheep
30. Sheep
31. Sheep

HARVEST TIME

Beloved, now we are children of God; and it has not yet been revealed what we shall be, but we know that when He is revealed, we shall be like Him, for we shall see Him as He is.

—1 John 3:2

My father was always interested, as a parent, to see how I would turn out. More than a few have called me a plain boy, and some have had the temerity to call me a fat one, but none of that matters. It is what I shall be in the spiritual harvest time that is critical. My prospects are extremely promising! He is the One who is Altogether Lovely, and I shall be like Him.

——— LORD OF THE HARVEST, ———

We thank You that we are in a state of change. We are daily becoming more like Jesus. We desire to see Him, knowing that when we do, we shall be like Him.

Brothers and Sisters

It is good neither to eat meat nor drink wine nor do anything by which your brother stumbles or is offended or is made weak.

—Romans 14:21

The temper of the times conspires to separate us from a sense of Christian community. We are encouraged to live for ourselves, and to ignore the effect of our actions upon our brothers and sisters in the Lord. Take care, lest we bruise the tender conscience, or corrupt the purity of fragile new faith. Our forbearing considerations now will be lavishly rewarded by our Judge in that day when He may say to us, "Well done."

Tender Lord,

We thank You for Your patience and kindness toward us. We are prone to every failing, yet You are forbearing with our weakness. Help us to be the same with those about us.

FALL COLORS

...to an inheritance incorruptible and undefiled and that does not fade away, reserved in heaven for you,

—1 Peter 1:4

We live in the autumn of life. We have witnessed the passing away of whole generations. Now, the mirror betrays that we also suffer a vanished tone and tint. We are no strangers to fading. Our strength was that of ten men, but now our vigor is abated, and our might has waned. The roses have left our cheeks, and the silver laces our hair. Isn't it good to know that some things do not fade away?

——— HEAVENLY TREASURE, ———

Many of the things that we would hold are slipping from our grasp. The day is near when we will part from all things. Teach us to value heavenly treasures which do not fade.

FLEXIBILITY

So the Lord said to him, "Arise and go to the street called Straight, and inquire at the house of Judas for one called Saul of Tarsus, for behold, he is praying.

—Acts 9:11

Imagine what was going on in the mind of our friend Ananias. Saul's was a name that he knew. Some Christians who had gone to see Saul never came back. Yet Ananias was flexible. Sometimes the Lord shows His grace to folks that we think are undeserving. If the truth were known, don't you think that there were those who thought the same about us? If only the worthy were called, there would be a lot of elbowroom in heaven.

—— LOVING FATHER, ——

We are amazed that You loved us, and purposed to lift us from the mire that was our habitation. Let us then brave any peril, that we might be found worthy of Your love.

FALL COLORS

I have been young, and now am old; yet I have not seen the righteous forsaken, nor his descendants begging bread.

—Psalms 37:25

I taught an assembly of high school students a while back. How bright were their young faces! In my unguarded thoughts, it seemed to me that I was one of them. How quickly has spring turned to fall! By the grace of God, I was able to bring them an encouraging word: God does not fail! His blessings extend to the generations of the righteous. It is an added boon to know that our obedience benefits our seed also.

——— OUR PORTION AND OUR PEACE, ———
Our earliest memories are of Your faithfulness. When in our long lives have You ever failed in Your promises? Give us zeal to tell of Your constancy toward us.

GRIEF

But I do not want you to be ignorant, brethren, concerning those who have fallen asleep, lest you sorrow as others who have no hope.

—1 Thessalonians 4:13

These words are for the children of God. The world sorrows, and they have grounds for it. They will appropriate these very words, but one can see from our text that they have no right. The soul of the departed Christian is already with the Lord. The body will be resurrected at the last day. The grief of today is swallowed up by the bright promises of tomorrow. There are tears to be sure, but not without hope!

———— RESURRECTED SAVIOR, ————

In these days when losses come daily, it is good for us to meditate upon Your empty tomb. Your rising is the firstfruit of all who sleep in You.

HARVEST TIME

The days of our lives are seventy years; and if by reason of strength they are eighty years, yet their boast is only labor and sorrow; for it is soon cut off, and we fly away.

—Psalms 90:10

All of our lives, we have been aware of the reapers work. He harvested the rows ahead. Sometimes he would take from the rank of youth, but usually he did not intrude into our generation. Now we stand in the first rank, and listen to the sweep of his blade. More years may be ours. They are likely to be laden with sorrows. Oh Lord, quiet our hearts, and bring us gently into Your sweet rest!

—— LORD OF THE HARVEST, ——

You have taught us not to fear the approach of death. You have promised to see us safely over Jordan. Now be our comfort as the time draws near.

Endings

"And God will wipe away every tear from their eyes; there shall be no more death, nor sorrow, nor crying. There shall be no more pain, for the former things have passed away."

—Revelation 21:4

We have let go of much in our long lives. People and things have been released back to the dust. This verse, then, brings comfort to the soul. We will wipe the tears from our eyes one last time. On the other side of that threshold we will never again say goodbye, never again stand a mournful watch through the long night, never again grieve over an empty place. These things, also, have an end. Through Christ, we will outlive them!

——— Tender Lord, ———

We thank You that we are not citizens of this world only. Therefore we do not grieve overmuch at the passing of dear ones. By Your grace, we will meet them again.

FORGIVENESS

> "And God will wipe away every tear from their eyes; there shall be no more death, nor sorrow, nor crying. There shall be no more pain, for the former things have passed away."
>
> —Revelation 21:4

This is a tender scene. We have been enemies of God but are now comforted by a loving Father. We have caused much sorrow and have ourselves shed so many tears. There has been many a night when sleep would not come for the pain that we bore, and that which we had inflicted on others. We shall see the end of it! Then we will know the joys of forgiveness, and have no further need to forgive!

——— FORGIVING FATHER, ———

We rejoice that all of our sin was put on Christ. Not just the dark things of yesterday, but also those things that our flesh may lead us into tomorrow.

GIVING

Yes, the Lord will give what is good ...
—Psalms 85:12

I'm glad that it is God who decides what is good. We are so weak and unspiritual that our choices would only bring troubles. He chooses not only what, but also when. In our haste, we would ask for a watch before we could tell the time. Out of His perfection, He gives us the very best. His gifts to us are timely. They arrive when we can most appreciate them, and when they bring Him the greatest glory.

———— GIVING LORD, ————

We would that we always ask within the frame of Your will. We are frail and stupid. We ever ask amiss. Help us to seek eternal things.

HARVEST TIME

...who once were not a people but are now the people of God, who had not obtained mercy but now have obtained mercy.

—1 Peter 2:10

There is much written and spoken of in our day about justice. Everybody demands it. As between God and myself, I was never very eager for it. It always seemed in my best interest that I should have mercy instead. It is not as though I did not do the calculation. Grace showed me my true merit. At harvest time, let me be hid in Jesus. I will plead His merit and not my own.

—— LORD OF THE HARVEST, ——

We praise You for the perfection of Your justice. We are glad that we are not the objects of it, but Christ has taken our punishment instead. Help us to rest in this truth.

FALL COLORS

Then Moses went up from the plains of Moab to Mount Nebo, to the top of Pisgah, which is across from Jericho. And the Lord showed him all the land …

— Deuteronomy 34:1

He is almost the last leaf. A chill wind blows as Moses makes this journey. Here he will mark an end. But, note the goodness of the Father. He allows Moses to see, as it were, the fruit of his labor. Behind are glittering triumphs, and some dismal failures. The work has wearied, and the task been thankless, but oh, the glory! Pause and rejoice that God will cause others to harvest the seed that you have planted.

——— GOOD AND GENTLE SAVIOR, ———

You have not called us to win. Our job is to run, and fight, and finish. Take the works of our hands and use them for Your glory, for all our good is of Your grace.

HEAVEN

After these things the word of the Lord came to Abram in a vision, saying, "Do not be afraid, Abram. I am your shield, your exceedingly great reward."

—Genesis 15:1

Heaven is a beacon to the Christian. In dark hours, when sorrows flood upon us, and this world is devoid of comfort, our soul's eye is drawn there. Yet it is not golden streets, or jasper walls that beguile, and allure. If heaven were that, and no more, our spirits would languish there. It is the Lord that is our very great reward. There is no heaven without Him.

——— HEAVENLY FATHER, ———

Like our father Abram, we have been pilgrims in this land. We are careful not to drive our roots too deep, for this is not our home. You are our destination and our reward.

HOLINESS

So those that entered, male and female of all flesh, went in as God had commanded him; and the Lord shut him in.

—Genesis 7:16

Outside, the thunder rolls out across the liquid landscape, and the cries of the forsaken can be heard as they claw and beg for entry. Can you imagine the occupants pressed to the walls and door? Do they strain to be just as near to death as they can? Or do you see them eager to be as near the center of safety as possible? Why do we then, being safe in Christ, always seek to be so near the world?

—— HOLY FATHER, ——

Help us to purge ourselves of sin so that we may be nearer the center of Your fellowship. We have no duty, or joy that exceeds our need to be like You.

RELATIONSHIPS

Beloved, if God so loved us, we also ought to love one another.

—1 John 4:11

I like to think that the older I grow, the more lovable I become. I am frequently amazed that everyone does not have affection for me. When I consider that Christ fixed His eye on me while I was yet a sinner, and His determined enemy, I am astounded by grace. If He can love me, then certainly I can love the unlovely in my acquaintance. In doing so, I become like Jesus. That brings glory to Him.

 DEAR FATHER, ———

Purge us of our foolish pride. Do not let us hold ourselves to be above another. When You found us, we were all sinners. There is a great equality in that.

EXPERIENCE

And we know that all things work together for good to those who love God, to those who are the called according to His purpose.

—Romans 8:28

From the vantage point of years, we appreciate the truth of this verse. There were hard times when it seemed that the sun would never shine again. There were sorrows so deep that words would not come. Only groanings could express the profound hurt and confusion of those hours. When only God could hear our voices, He drew us near. We could not walk as close to Him, except for the experience of those times.

——— BENEVOLENT SAVIOR, ———

You have promised to work all things for our good. The things themselves may not be good, but when they are done, we will be better for them.

HARVEST TIME

Then he threw down the pieces of silver in the temple and departed, and went and hanged himself.

—Matthew 27:5

It was a horrific end, but one that was well deserved. Though he was the beneficiary of manifold kindnesses and the eyewitness to miracles, Judas would betray the hand that held every hope. Sin and rebellion have a harvest, and Judas is gathered in it. Every soul, look here and fear. Satan would not love you if he could. Mercy and grace may be found in Christ alone. Better that you had found mercy yesterday, but there is no better time than today.

——— LORD OF THE HARVEST, ———

Your justice will harvest all men. In that day, we pray that You will hide us in the Rock of Ages. There will be shelter there for our souls.

JOY

Therefore with joy you will draw water from the wells of salvation.

—Isaiah 12:3

We have been many years in the way. There have been dry places when we thought we should die. Then by the prompting of grace we come upon a fountain. It is new to us, but we drink deeply from it and it refreshes. Note that we must draw the water from these deeps. When we are most in need, we ought to be most in study and prayer. God will not leave us parched and dry.

———— FOUNTAIN OF ALL JOYS, ————

We praise You for the deep fountains that we find in Your love, Word, and mercy. These are rich and overflowing, giving life and joy to whosoever will drink.

Fall Colors

> They are clouds without water, carried about
> by the winds; late autumn trees without fruit,
> twice dead, pulled up by the roots;
>
> —Jude 1:12

Pray that these words will not be so of us! The day is ending and we have no fruit! How can it be that in these many years we have yielded no profit? If that is true of us, what can we do? We have not yet been pulled up! While the sun still shines upon us, we may bring forth an increase. We hold no promise of another day. Bestir yourself then, that the harvest may yet be plentiful.

——— Longsuffering Lord, ———

We fear to come to our end without fruit. Bestir us today to much labor for the Kingdom. Let our entry there be joyous—bringing many sheaves.

PASSING IT ON

And He said to them, "Go into all the world and preach the gospel to every creature.
—Mark 16:15

How my soul gives thanks for the Lord's command to pass it on! I was not among the first rank of those that stood to hear the truth. All of the rich and influential would have had claim on the preaching of the good news before it might have come to my ear. Because it must be preached to all, it came, also, to me in the low, and dark places. Thank God that the gospel is for all creatures!

——— TRIUMPHANT LORD, ———

We are included in "every creature." If this were not so, it might never have come to some to us. We thank You that we are comprehended in Your love.

TRIUMPH

Therefore He says: "When He ascended on high, he led captivity captive, and gave gifts to men."

—Ephesians 4:8

As with the conquers of old, Christ makes a great display of the spoils of His great battle in the triumph over sin. He has in His victory vanguard, those who did sorely oppress His people. He has bound them and rendered them impotent to do us harm. He displays them openly so that we might never again fear them. The sin under which we labored hard years can no longer have dominion over us.

——— VICTORIOUS CHRIST, ———

You have won the great triumph. Sin is vanquished and we are free. Help us to enter into Your victory by having the greatest contempt for the evil that You have defeated.

GLEANING

And her mother-in-law said to her, "Where have you gleaned today? And where did you work?

—Ruth 2:19

As we live our lives, little pieces from the places we go, the things we think, see, read, and experience remain in our minds and become a part of us. There is a caution in this, and also, great opportunities. Be wary of physical or mental visits to places whose gleanings will hurt our soul. Ask the Lord to direct your paths to venues that will bless the present, and remain to hallow another day as well.

——— WATCHFUL FATHER, ———

We thank You that Your Word is a light for our path. Keep us from straying out of Your way. Help us to mind our brother's path along with ours.

MOVING

And they stoned Stephen as he was calling on God and saying, "Lord Jesus, receive my spirit."

—Acts 7:59

Sometimes, when I really ought to be engaged in other pursuits, I allow my mind to muse as to the time and circumstances of my "moving day." Somehow, I do not find myself desiring to be stoned. I want to be loved by all and missed by most. It is really better, however, to be as Stephen. The last thing in this world that Stephen saw was a rock. He opened his eyes in heaven, and beheld the Rock of Ages.

—— HEAVENLY FATHER, ——

Cause us to be bold in our witness. Let us care nothing for the enemies that oppose us. Bring us into Your Kingdom in triumph.

RELATIONSHIPS

And let us consider one another in order to stir up love and good works,

—Hebrews 10:24

There are lots of people who love to stir things up. I must confess that, on occasion, I am one of these. It is a pleasure of advancing age to throw a nugget into the fire and watch the young folk dig it out. I ought, however, to be setting an example of good works for the next generation. They should be challenged to match my love for the brethren, and to emulate my zeal for the lost.

——— DEAR FATHER, ———

Help us to be an example to the young. Let our example light a thousand candles that we may confound the growing darkness with Your truth.

SIMPLIFICATION

Thus Midian was subdued before the children of Israel, so that they lifted their heads no more. And the country was quiet for forty years in the days of Gideon.

—Judges 8:28

These are triumphal words, but they must be prefaced by a sad story. Israel had lived for many years in fear of these people. They came every year like hoards of locusts to devour Israel's crops and abuse its citizens. All of this occurred while Israel had the Lord's commitment that He would go before them in battle. What looked very complex to them was really simple. All they needed was to act on the clear promise of God.

——— LOVING FATHER, ———

We thank You for Your many and kind promises. Help us to study Your Word so that we may know the wealth of good that You intend for us.

VALUES

Then all the rulers said to all the congregation, "We have sworn to them by the Lord God of Israel; now therefore, we may not touch them."
—Joshua 9:19

I miss the days when one could count on a handshake and a promise. In our verse, the Israelite leadership have gotten themselves into a fix. They were misled into giving their word. Foolishly, they swore by the Lord without having all the facts. Now, in the face of severe criticism by their brothers, and hard evidence of deception, they hold fast to their promise. I love them for their steadfastness. I respect their example to us.

—— RIGHTEOUS FATHER, ——

We praise You for Your purity. We confess that we are given to a lying tongue and carelessness of word and purpose. Help us to be more like You.

FALL COLORS

Now Abraham was one hundred years old when his son Isaac was born to him.

—Genesis 21:5

Here is our father Abraham in the autumn of his life. It is a time when he might reasonably have thought of giving up tent life, and perhaps buy a little time-share over on the coast. But, God does not intend that either Sarah, or Abraham should rest. Few things will disrupt a plan of retirement like the birth of a child. Perhaps, in the plan of God, fresh, unusual, or unexpected blessings are headed our way too.

——— KINDLY LORD, ———

Surprise us today with some unexpected good. Or, if it be Your will, place us in the midst of some unplanned trial. In all things, show us Your glory.

WAGING THE BATTLE

"Wherever you hear the sound of the trumpet, rally to us there. Our God will fight for us."
—Nehemiah 4:20

I had tremendous advantages as a child. One of these is the fact that I had a big brother. When one is eight years old, a thirteen-year-old brother is a definite equalizer in any fray. I liked having the "ultimate weapon" on my side. The Christian is in a similar position. The world will gather all its formidable forces against us. But, we need never be afraid. He is the source of all power. He will win our victory.

——— SHIELD AND DEFENDER, ———

The battle for the right still rages. Help us to bring honor to Your name in the conflict. Help us to see beyond the warfare. Let our eyes behold Your glorious and eternal peace.

Sheep

All we like sheep have gone astray; we have turned, every one, to his own way; and the Lord has laid on Him the iniquity of us all.

—Isaiah 53:6

It's interesting to notice that each and every sheep went its own way. Yet, all of them went astray. One might conclude then, that without a Shepherd all of them would have died, for none went in the right direction. In this, we see our desperate condition. Every spiritual choice that we have made outside of Christ has been wrong! The product of our error would surely have been death except He intercepted our souls and brought us to safety.

——— O Lord, ———

How can we ever render sufficient thanks to You? In the darkest night, You have sought us out! From the greatest peril, You have saved us! Blessed be Your name.

SHEEP

"And when he comes home, he calls together his friends and neighbors, saying to them, 'Rejoice with me, for I have found my sheep which was lost!'"

—Luke 15:6

I had a colleague years ago who had married into a family of Kansas sheepherders. When I asked him about the characteristics of sheep he responded, "Sheep are stupid." I know I am a sheep. This could distress me as I realize that these creatures can be lost and not know it. So it is with all sons of Adam. We would all wander and die except that the Good Shepherd has sought us and found us.

——— GOOD SHEPHERD, ———

We are so thankful that we are sheep of Your fold. We were lost and You found us. You picked us out of the mire, and will carry us all the way to heaven.

SHEEP

The wicked are estranged from the womb;
they go astray as soon as they are born,
speaking lies.

—Psalms 58:3

All of us sheep can relate to this truth. Every last ram and ewe among us was bent upon going astray at birth. We were lost and we were not seeking to be found. If Christ had not determined to love us and to find us, we would be lost still.

Sheep are so stupid that (if one could talk sheep talk) they would not know they were lost. If they did actually know, they would lie about it.

——— LORD, ———

Teach me to cease my wandering. Hold me so close that I cannot stray. Help me to see my need and to cleave to You, who are my only safety.

November

1. Fellowship
2. Homecoming
3. Fall Colors
4. Parting
5. Hard Work
6. Servanthood
7. Brothers and Sisters
8. A Full Quiver
9. Holiness
10. Waging the Battle
11. Beginnings
12. Images
13. Values
14. Celebration
15. Clutter
16. Grief
17. Heaven
18. Clutter
19. Thanksgiving
20. Thanksgiving
21. Thanksgiving
22. Thanksgiving
23. Thanksgiving
24. Thanksgiving
25. Thanksgiving
26. Relationships
27. Heaven
28. Images
29. Joy
30. Heaven

FELLOWSHIP

...and sent Timothy, our brother and minister of God, and our fellow laborer in the gospel of Christ, to establish you and encourage you concerning your faith,

—1 Thessalonians 3:2

"Dad, can I drive the car?" "Yes, son, I believe you can if you really want to," was my father's sober reply. Our fellowship was like that. He never failed to encourage me. It was a time before automatic transmissions. Repeated stalls, spine jarring jerks, and the smell of burnt rubber did not daunt him. Our encouragement of fellow Christians is necessary to their growth. In this, our pilgrim journey, it will sure help if some of us can drive.

—— EVERLASTING FATHER, ——

The memories of love flood in upon us. We recall those whom You have sent to minister to us. Help us to do unto others, as has been so sweetly done for us.

Homecoming

So he died in a good old age, full of days
and riches and honor; and Solomon his son
reigned in his place.

—1 Chronicles 29:28

Who among us would not sign up to have this epitaph apply to us? David was full of days, not years. This suggests that he lived each of them. A lot of rich people are not honorable, but David was. God blessed him with an able son. Solomon would reign in his father's stead. The richness and blessing that lay upon David in his last day pales into triviality as compared to opulence and glory of his homecoming.

Heavenly Father,

Help us to put our affairs in good order. Let us leave no slight unforgiven, nor any duty untended. Let us pass with honor so that Your name will be praised.

FALL COLORS

He has made everything beautiful in its time ...

—Ecclesiastes 3:11

The sun shines with special brilliance in the fall. The rustle of incrementally cooler breezes wrests the tender leaves from their branches, and they fall to form a carpet of breathtaking color. In this, there is a hidden beauty. The seeds of a future spring are scattered by the approach of this season of rest. The advance of chilling cold betokens a splendid resurrection when each shall come forth again with greater splendor and enhanced glory.

——— CREATOR AND SUSTAINER, ———

We see the change of seasons that You faithfully bring about. They are a beautiful reminder of Your constancy and goodness. We worship You for that.

PARTING

Depart from me, you evildoers, for I will keep the commandments of my God!

—Psalms 119:115

We are self-deluding if we think that we can be the same after an encounter with saving grace. The old gang will be content to abandon us soon enough. Somehow we just will not be as much fun as formerly. For our part, we will not find the same satisfaction from the old faces. Yesterday's haunts will lack present appeal. Keeping the Lord's commandments will divide us from the old group. The parting will be by mutual agreement.

——— KINDLY LORD. ———

We thank You that You did not leave us as You found us. We are pleased to be parted from the old life, and we will never stop thanking You for the new.

Hard Work

So it was, whenever Israel had sown, Midianites would come up; also Amalekites and the people of the East would come up against them.

—Judges 6:3

In the course of my travels, I have been blessed to meet farmers. They are a hardworking and devoted group, but oddly, to little purpose, for I never met one that was having a good year. Much worse off were the Israelites referenced in our verse. They planted, but were never able to reap because God sent others to steal their harvest because of sin. It will be so with us until we learn that there is no prosperity without obedience.

———— Patient Lord, ————

We are a silly people. We delude ourselves that we can live outside Your law and flourish. Show us that we can only find prosperity in obedience.

SERVANTHOOD

Paul, a bondservant of Jesus Christ, called to be an apostle, separated to the gospel of God...
—Romans 1:1

Paul is the servant of Christ because he is under a great obligation to Him. He was blind and he was given sight. He was bent upon his own ruin, and was turned around. Paul was determined to destroy, and became a builder. He had busied himself with bringing tidings of arrest, and death, but was transformed to become the bearer of the blessed good news of the gospel. His debt was great, his mission blessed, and his end glorious.

——— TENDER LORD, ———

We are overwhelmed with the magnitude of our debt to You. We pray that You help us to see our obligation to serve. Give us grace to do that with joy.

BROTHERS AND SISTERS

...no longer as a slave but more than a slave-- a beloved brother, especially to me but how much more to you, both in the flesh and in the Lord.

—Philemon 1:16

How level is the Gospel field! Upon the ground of grace, Christian brothers and sisters know no difference of caste or distinction of social standing. Onesimus was an escaped slave, but Paul returned this erring one to his Christian master: He is a brother now. Take him in and love him. He will be faithful in service to you because he is loyal to Christ. How may we, the objects of grace, exalt ourselves over another?

——— PATIENT SAVIOR, ———

We are prone to exalt ourselves above our brothers and sisters. Teach us to be lowly and meek, since everything that we have and are is a gift from Your hand.

A FULL QUIVER

Now we, brethren, as Isaac was, are children
of promise.

—Galatians 4:28

I have been, in the course of my life, both a son, and a stepson. It is better to be a son. It is important to note that in the many references to the beneficiaries of grace, we are all identified as children. This is a comfort to me. God has no stepchildren. There are no grandchildren for that matter. We stand upon a great and level ground of grace. Let that concept comfort your soul.

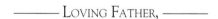

——— LOVING FATHER, ———

We will have an eternity to think about Your goodness to us. You have brought us into Your family. We do not deserve that. It is by Your grace, and we love You for it.

HOLINESS

Give to the Lord the glory due His name;
bring an offering, and come before Him. Oh,
worship the Lord in the beauty of holiness!
—1 Chronicles 16:29

In a world such as ours, where much has degenerated to the gross and vile, it is good to recall the beauties of holiness. They are seen in the submission of children to parents. Beauty abounds in a whispered, "Thank you." They bedew the faces of mutually pledged lovers. They trail the path of the dutiful minister. They are in the peace that graces the face of the departed saint. To desire such beauty is to desire Christ.

——— HOLY FATHER, ———

We are wrapped in a world of beauty. We have beheld the beauty of Your earthly creation. But, spiritual scenes excel all others. Let us see the beauties of Your holiness.

WAGING THE BATTLE

Now these are the nations which the Lord left, that He might test Israel by them, that is, all who had not known any of the wars in Canaan.

—Judges 3:1

The great issues of history do not change. The players vary, as does the geography, but darkness always rages against the light, and sin always opposes righteousness. We are not to sit on the sidelines as this battle rages. The Lord will test us. He knows the outcome. But, He tests us that we might emerge strengthened and matured. We may have as much of the spiritual Promised Land as we will take, use, and defend.

——— GOD WITH US, ———

The battle is long, and we are likely to faint unless You bear us up. You are our strength and our salvation. Bring us at last safely into Your wonderful peace.

BEGINNINGS

"Of gold and silver and bronze and iron there is no limit. Arise and begin working, and the Lord be with you."

—1 Chronicles 22:16

Most of us have known lives that continually contend with limitations. We have not enough money, too little time, and an insufficient budget. We must grasp the reality that it need not be so in our spiritual lives. God, who is the fountain of all resources, will not withhold anything from us. However, what use to us is a spiritual watch if we have not yet learned to tell time? Begin working. Our day may be short.

——— BOUNTIFUL FATHER, ———

Open our eyes that we may see the bounty of Your provision. You are an infinite God who will not withhold any good gift from us.

Images

> And He said to them, "Whose image and inscription is this?" They said to Him, "Caesar's." And He said to them, "Render therefore to Caesar the things that are Caesar's, and to God the things that are God's."
>
> —Matthew 22:20, 21

Our father Adam was made in the image of God. We have been busy over these millennia in an attempt to efface the imprint that God has put upon us. But try as we will, it is a part of our fallen misery that we cannot behave as befits the mark of our Maker. We are His representation. We owe Him our admiration, loyalty, obedience, and love. Let us render to God those things that belong to Him.

——— Immutable Father, ———

We are wont to give ourselves to lesser gods—ones that we have made with our hands or minds. Take us and mold us into Your likeness.

VALUES

I was in the Spirit on the Lord's Day ...
—Revelation 1:10

I remember when America was at least nominally Christian. Those who did not attend church on Sunday at least stayed in—so as not to be seen by their neighbors. The Lord is a free-flowing fountain of mercy. The country, generally, and its citizens individually perish for want of that pardon which only comes from God by the gospel. We are unlikely to hear the good news of His grace while slopping barbecue sauce on a rack of ribs.

—————— FORGIVING FATHER, ——————

We are a presumptuous people. You would be just to exterminate us and bestow Your love on others. Please turn us from our carelessness and back to Your law.

CELEBRATION

Oh, sing to the Lord a new song! For He has done marvelous things; his right hand and His holy arm have gained Him the victory.

—*Psalms 98:1*

I have been long in the race. I am, from time to time, battered by the fight. But I am not called to win, but to run. I must fight, but I may not ever see the victory. This is cause for celebration. Responsibility for the triumph would be too heavy for me. Victory is certain. I need have no concern because God will win it. I can find repose on the pillow of that truth.

——— TRIUMPHANT FATHER, ———

The battle is long. We desire to see the end, but we know that it may not come in our day. Still we sleep the sleep of assurance because the victory is in Your hands.

CLUTTER

...casting down arguments and every high thing that exalts itself against the knowledge of God, bringing every thought into captivity to the obedience of Christ,

—2 Corinthians 10:5

This business of following Christ is no easy thing. We have disciplined our bodies so that they are "no shows" at the old worldly haunts. But, what can be done about our minds? A thousand wayward thoughts zip in and out of our conscious. We need a gatekeeper. Let us use God's word like one of those measuring sticks they use for amusement park rides. If it doesn't meet God's standards, it doesn't get in.

——— FAITHFUL KEEPER, ———

We are like sheep. We go astray at every crossroad. We would never be so wise as to return to Your care except that You seek us out and bring us back into Your fold.

GRIEF

Surely He has borne our griefs and carried our sorrows; yet we esteemed Him stricken, smitten by God, and afflicted.

—Isaiah 53:4

The point will be missed if we fail to understand that they were our griefs. This bright star of heaven's glory ought not to have ever known other than richly deserved joy. He entered into sorrow for His people. He knew derision, pain, falsity, abandonment, even death. He bore all of these outrages, which rightly ought to have fallen on us, with silence and patience. He gladly endured the stripes that we might be healed.

——— WONDERFUL SAVIOR, ———

Help us to see that You have born our griefs, and carried our sorrows. That being so, teach us to leave these with You, that we may be free to love and serve You more.

Heaven

"And being in torments in Hades, he lifted up his eyes and saw Abraham afar off, and Lazarus in his bosom."

—Luke 16:23

Imagine a society where there is no crime. There are no locks upon the doors. Everyone that you meet loves you, and treats you as you would want to be treated. Pain has no place there, nor does darkness, or want. It is into this scene that the rich man gazes. He may look, but may not enter. As I let my mind run on this, I can't help but believe that this is a major factor in making hell unbearable.

——— Heavenly Father, ———

Set our eyes upon Your rest. Let everything else fade from our desires. We would be there because You are there. This is our comfort on the long journey.

CLUTTER

That very day Pilate and Herod became friends with each other, for previously they had been at enmity with each other.

—Luke 23:12

I have been in my share of scrapes. One wonders how much fewer they might have been if I had exercised better judgment in choosing chums. Bad friends are clutter that wall us off from grace. Godly companions are now much to my advantage. They help to deflect my soul from sin, and spur me to good works. The fates of Pilate and Herod would have been vastly different had they chosen to befriend Christ rather than one another.

——— FAITHFUL FRIEND, ———

We have no truer friend than You. You would have us save our souls. We need to be more like You by ridding ourselves of all that hinders our fellowship.

Thanksgiving Reflections

That I may proclaim with the voice of thanksgiving, and tell of all Your wondrous works.

—Psalms 26:7

There is a time in the life of a child when there are no troubles. Not that there were no cares at all, they just weren't my worries. If there was a better cook than my mother, I had no knowledge of it. Early Thanksgivings are blessed because they are enjoyed in safety and warmth. We might delight in those again if we could appreciate, by faith, the security and love that is ours in Christ.

——— O Great Provision, ———

We thank You that we need never be poor threatened cold or unloved. You have suffered all of these for our sakes. Let us proclaim Your wonderful works to the nations.

THANKSGIVING REFLECTIONS

I will praise the name of God with a song, and will magnify Him with thanksgiving.
—Psalms 69:30

I remember old-fashioned Thanksgivings spent with godly relatives in the South. They would gather from afar. Many had traveled long miles on country roads comprised of two ruts in the red earth. Many visitors would, after much pleading, spend the night. The holiday would end with the singing of hymns, and loving hugs all around. Some have memories of more opulent surroundings. Doubtless, others enjoyed finer and richer fare. But, none were purer, sweeter, or nearer to the heart of God.

——— LOVING PROVIDER, ———

Father You have laded us with every luxury all of our long lives. We have failed You but You have ever been constant toward us. Accept our gratefulness and thanksgiving.

THANKSGIVING REFLECTIONS

Continue earnestly in prayer, being vigilant in it with thanksgiving;

—Colossians 4:2

Our lives should be one long prayer of thanksgiving. Our sense of obligation would be heightened if we had a better understanding of what we deserve. We were aliens to the people of God. We were actual enemies of our Creator. He has all power, and might have at any time meted out to us what we actually deserved. Our sense of obligation will engender a love that cannot be contained. It must burst forth in thanksgiving.

——— BOUNTIFUL FATHER, ———

How we praise You for Your forbearance. We might have been banished from Your face and Your grace. But You have lavished Your love upon us. We thank You for that.

Thanksgiving Reflections

"And when you offer a sacrifice of thanksgiving to the Lord, offer it of your own free will."

—Leviticus 22:29

The Lord knows the heart of man. It is as transparent to Him as clear glass. He cannot be fooled by mere outward acts. If the heart does not follow the deed, our compliance to His law is unacceptable. The demands of God relative to our thanksgiving are reasonable. We do not have one thing that was not given to us by Him. If that does not excite gratitude in our hearts, then we are the most ungrateful of creatures.

———— Precious Father, ————

All of our long lives we have eaten from Your hand. You have withheld no good thing from us. Let us never cease to praise Your name in thanksgiving.

THANKSGIVING REFLECTIONS

Thus says the Lord: "Stand in the ways and see, and ask for the old paths, where the good way is, and walk in it; then you will find rest for your souls. But they said, 'We will not walk in it.'

—Jeremiah 6:16

When I was a youth, the existence of a Creator was not a matter of general doubt. When Thanksgiving Day came, we offered up prayers of gratitude to God in confidence. We knew that He heard us and was pleased to hear our thanks. In this new millennium, we continue the form, but the substance has gone from it. For me and mine, we will walk in the old paths. We find rest for the soul there.

——— PRINCE OF PEACE, ———

Mankind is a sea that constantly roils for want of peace. Every wind drives them and many currents carry them. Lord, help us to patiently bear the message of peace.

THANKSGIVING REFLECTIONS

And the Lord God prepared a plant and made it come up over Jonah, that it might be shade for his head to deliver him from his misery. So Jonah was very grateful for the plant.

—Jonah 4:6

Jonah had issues. He was upset with God that He had been the vehicle of mercy to a people that he thought to be unworthy. He had a stingy little heart. See, however, the goodness and patience of the Father. He caused a plant to grow up and shade him while he fretted. Wouldn't it be better for the Jonahs amongst us, if we simply trusted God to do the right thing, and then be thankful for it?

———— PATIENT FATHER, ————

Because of our sin we have no means to know the patience that You have shown to us. Forgive the smallness of our hearts, and enlarge our thanks by Your grace.

THANKSGIVING REFLECTIONS

Let us come before His presence with thanksgiving; let us shout joyfully to Him with psalms.

—Psalms 95:2

The world is eager to go anywhere and do anything for pleasure. All the while, they have an affect of elation. There is no real jubilation, however, that does not have an element of thanksgiving to God. He is the author of all joy. If we experience delight, we are the objects of His undeserved goodness. If we do not acknowledge that, then we ought to wipe some of those big smiles off our faces.

—— LORD, ——

You are the source of our gladness and thanksgiving. Life will wrest from us every other joy. Only those that are experienced in thankfulness honor and glorify You.

RELATIONSHIPS

Husbands, love your wives, just as Christ also loved the church and gave Himself for her,
— Ephesians 5:25

Except for our relationship to the Savior, there can be no closer bond on this earth than that which is between husband and wife. Love has many meanings. We might be left to wonder just how it is intended here, except that an example is given which brooks no misunderstanding. Husbands are to love wives sacrificially. They are to love their spouse more than life. Can any wife have a legitimate fear in this relationship?

DEAR FATHER,

We wonder at Your love for us. We are amazed that for sake of it You submitted to the cross. Kindle a similar affection within us that we may love another above our own life.

HEAVEN

After these things I looked, and behold, a great multitude which no one could number, of all nations, tribes, peoples, and tongues, standing before the throne and before the Lamb, clothed with white robes, with palm branches in their hands,

—Revelation 7:9

See the children of God. They are a great multitude. They have come through oceans of blood, and have trodden the winepress of this world's hatred, and wrath. There was no friendly voice, nor did any extend kindness. They were reckoned as dead, and no room was ever made for them. But, look now. Whatever the cost, it is repaid here. The hope of every cold, and sleepless night is realized, and they are safe at home.

——— HEAVENLY FATHER, ———

Like Moses, we have counted the cost, and considered the reward. How eager we are now to get on toward home.

IMAGES

"You shall have no other gods before Me."
—Exodus 20:3

Typically we think here of the pathetic little images that men are wont to make. They would hold these close and bow down to them. While this is certainly included in the commandment, we must also consider those things that we would love before our love for God. Our Lord is a jealous God. He will not tolerate competition. We must love Him above spouse, children, summer cottage, position, money, or thing. He must be first in all.

———— IMMUTABLE FATHER, ————

Purify our loves, and help us to prioritize them. Let us put away those that dishonor our standing as children, and cause us to love You above all.

JOY

Yet I will rejoice in the Lord, I will joy in the God of my salvation.

—Habakkuk 3:18

The day has wearied us. We have not succeeded. Our enemies seem to be on the increase. Health has failed. Loneliness has supplanted friendship. Those who were best loved by us have fallen to the reapers scythe. Our worldly journey is like this so that we should never become too attached and comfortable here. It is not our home. We must fix our eyes on heaven. The God of our salvation waits for us there.

——— FOUNTAIN OF ALL JOYS, ———

Where does the joy come from? We cannot find the cause for it in events. It is our knowledge of God that drives the tear away, and brings the smile to our lips.

HEAVEN

For our citizenship is in heaven, from which we also eagerly wait for the Savior, the Lord Jesus Christ,

—Philemon 3:20

No matter how bleak or inhospitable a place may seem, those who are citizens will speak highly of it. I love the place of my birth, but my soul's roots are not there. Instead, my thoughts have lately been of heaven. Mother and father wait. Theirs and a thousand other faded voices draw me along the homeward path. I will soon see Jesus. The hour grows late and my soul is full.

——— HEAVENLY FATHER, ———

We are from another place. However beautiful, we have had a brief glimpse of heaven, and can no more be satisfied here. Show us the way home.

December

EXPERIENCE

The bin of flour was not used up, nor did the jar of oil run dry, according to the word of the Lord which He spoke by Elijah.

—1 Kings 17:16

There have been times in our lives when the cupboard was pretty bare. I remember in college when my young wife and I would share a plate of buttered noodles for our supper. In her cheery way she would say, "Some day we'll look back on this and laugh." Though at the time I thought it unlikely, I am pleased to say that now the memories are dear. Experience tells me that little is much if God is with us.

——— FAITHFUL PROVIDER, ———

We have known You these many years, and have had countless opportunities to test Your faithfulness. You have never let our cups run dry, nor was our flour consumed.

JOY

"His Lord said to him, 'Well done, good and faithful servant; you were faithful over a few things, I will make you ruler over many things. Enter into the joy of your Lord.'"

—Matthew 25:21

We mope about with long faces. It would seem that service to our Lord was the most wearisome of occupations. If we suffer persecution, we are likely never to get over it. We have lost sight of our joy. God Himself is our reward! From His throne flow rivers of pleasure. Get a grip on the truth. It is just a few more days and then we shall enter fully into Him. That will be joy forever.

——— FOUNTAIN OF ALL JOYS, ———

We know not much of accolades in this world, though we have tried hard and worked long. But, oh the joy at the end of our days to hear You say "Well done!"

LOVE

But God demonstrates His own love toward us, in that while we were still sinners, Christ died for us.

—Romans 5:8

I remember scrubbing myself up, putting on my best clothes, combing my lush, black hair, and going out to meet my future wife. The theory was that if I could make myself appear to be clean, well mannered, and potentially successful, she might come to love me. This was not how God came to love us. There was no good, either potential or actual, in us. We were vile and without merit when Christ laid down His spotless life for us.

—— LOVING SAVIOR, ——

The thought chills our souls. How could we have lived in rebellion against You? Thank You for subduing our hearts, and causing them to beat for You.

OBEDIENCE

The eye that mocks his father, and scorns obedience to his mother, the ravens of the valley will pick it out, and the young eagles will eat it.

—Proverbs 30:17

One of the great tragedies of our day is that of children who will not obey parents. Errant voices tell us that we will warp budding personalities if we constrain them. The truth of God is that rebellious offspring are already warped. If they cannot be conformed to authority, they are prey. The world is full of vicious hunters who cannot feel real love. They will praise our children's defiance while readying a stroke that will slay them.

——— DEAR LORD, ———

We pray that You will keep our children from the stranger's way. Everywhere are those who would harm them. Build a wall around them so they cannot be brought to harm.

FAITH

Only let your conduct be worthy of the gospel of Christ, so that whether I come and see you or am absent, I may hear of your affairs, that you stand fast in one spirit, with one mind striving together for the faith of the gospel,

—Philemon 1:27

A product of faith is unity. Persons who truly believe will coalesce around the truth they hold. Let the heathen rage. Those who know nothing of Christ might well squabble. They have no basis to care for one another, and their father, the Devil cannot love them. But, our faith binds us together in Christ. Since we have no shortage of enemies, our oneness is essential if we are to advance the blessed gospel.

——— WORTHY LORD, ———

We pray when You look upon us that You find us in unity. What does it matter that worldly friends are few if we have You to uphold us?

BROTHERS AND SISTERS

A friend loves at all times, and a brother is born for adversity.

—Proverbs 17:17

I have two older brothers. I think that, as boys, they misunderstood this verse in that they seemed eager to bring adversity into my life. A better understanding would have been that in adversity, a friend becomes a brother. It has been a joy, and a refuge to have two such loving supportive people in my life. How Christ has multiplied this advantage! I have Christian brothers everywhere eager to love and care for me.

——— SAVIOR AND FRIEND, ———

We thank You for our Christian brothers and sisters. How wonderful it is that the most precious gift of this life is one we can take to heaven with us.

HEAVEN

...because of the hope which is laid up for you in heaven, of which you heard before in the word of the truth of the gospel,

—Colossians 1:5

I have a lot of hopes in this world. With the passage of years, it becomes apparent that many of these will never see fulfillment. I had hoped to be smarter and more handsome. Perhaps I might even have a full head of hair restored to me. These are trivial things as contrasted to the eternal hopes that are vested in heaven. Christ will be there and sin will not. Those hopes will get me on down the road today.

 HEAVENLY FATHER,

We have held the most earnest hopes in this world. Most have come to nothing. We have a hope that will not disappoint. We shall see You, and it will be enough.

REPENTANCE

Then the Lord said to him, "This is the land of which I swore to give Abraham, Isaac, and Jacob, saying, 'I will give it to your descendants.' I have caused you to see it with your eyes, but you shall not cross over there."
—Deuteronomy 34:4

We live in a soap opera world. We are persuaded that no matter the wrong done before the first commercial, everything will be righted by the end of the half hour. We might stretch our imagination to allow for a mini-series, but in the end, everything will be fine. Moses sinned against the Lord, and things could not be made right again in this world. Some things are done and cannot be undone. Learn from Moses' example.

—— FORGIVING SAVIOR, ——

Help us to see the immutable effect of our sin in this world. Steer us into a walk of righteousness, that we might avoid the irreparable ruin that follows evil.

Simplification

David fastened his sword to his armor, and he tried to walk, for he had not tested them. And David said to Saul, "I cannot walk with these, for I have not tested them." So David took them off.

—1 Samuel 17:39

He must have made a comic picture: this little lad attempting to walk in the king's armor. King Saul had the size but David had the heart. The boy soon decided that what he must do is simplify. Sometimes all that complicated solutions do is disable us. Goliath, the big fellow from Gath, was about to be bested by a ruddy youth, a humble sling, and a smooth stone. Recognition of our own weakness gives us strength with God.

——— Great Lord, ———

We thank You that Your strength surrounds us and protects us. Help us to see that we are weak in ourselves, but that we may be strong in Your might.

Relationships

"For whom the Lord loves He chastens, and scourges every son whom He receives."
—Hebrews 12:6

Generally, certainty is a good thing. There are times, however, when it nags at the fringes of our well-being. There was a level of offense in our home that was sure to bring my father's corrective action. He believed in a liberal application of the switch. Viewed from this distance of years, it is a sweet affirmation of my position as a son. There were a lot of wild boys in my old neighborhood. But, my father never whipped any of them.

——— Dear Father, ———
We thank You for our correction for it confirms our standing as children. You care for us and would see us know the joys of obedience.

ENDINGS

"The harvest is past, the summer is ended, and we are not saved!"

—Jeremiah 8:20

We are thankful that among the myriad of graces that God has provided, He has allocated a harvest time for the soul. You read these words in the midst of God's great gathering-in. Today, if you hear His calling, do not turn a deaf ear—for we understand from our text that the summertime of the soul has an ending. Find peace with God while the sun of His love still stands high in the heavens.

—— LORD OF THE HARVEST, ——

We thank You that when we were afar off, You sent Your gospel to us. We wait with patience, the great gathering-in. In that great day, let us be found in You.

CELEBRATION

"The Lord lives! Blessed be my Rock! Let God be exalted, the Rock of my salvation!"

—2 Samuel 22:47

As long as the Lord lives, we shall live also. In a world of change, we are founded upon a rock that cannot be moved, or broken. In these things, we celebrate the Lord. But most of all, we thank Him for drawing our souls out of the pit. He has put a song in our mouths and has given us a bright hope for the future. If sleep does not come tonight, ponder these things.

—— ROCK OF OUR SALVATION, ——

We thank You that our redemption is not based on anything that can be changed. You do not vary. Neither is there the least shadow of Your turning.

GLEANING

"Let her glean even among the sheaves, and do not reproach her."

—Ruth 2:15

The gospel goes out unto the whole field of mankind. It separates wheat from tares and binds the individual stalks together in sheaves. It is a rare privilege for the Christian to glean from among this harvest. While there may be real grain among the briars and weeds of the world, there are tares there also. There is no nourishment in them to sustain the soul. Stick close to the congregation of God's people. That is where the truth is concentrated.

—— WONDERFUL PROVIDER, ——

We thank You for the people of God. They will help us to stay close to the center of Your will. Give us the sense to find ourselves always among Your children.

PASSING IT ON

Also I heard the voice of the Lord, saying:
"Whom shall I send, and who will go for us?"
Then I said, "Here am I! Send me."

—Isaiah 6:8

Isaiah had just been privileged to see the Lord. On the strength of that experience, he was willing to go anywhere and do anything. It is important that anyone going out to do the Lord's work should share a glimpse of that vision. God cannot be thwarted, nor can His purposes be frustrated. His side is the winning side. If our witness is weak and faltering, perhaps it is because we need to see the Lord afresh.

——— TRIUMPHANT LORD, ———

Bring us afresh that vision of Your exalted greatness. When we are imbued with that, we will have courage to face any foe.

WINTER WARMTH

...in weariness and toil, in sleeplessness often, in hunger and thirst, in fastings often, in cold and nakedness...

—2 Corinthians 11:27

This time of year, we often get those attractive brochures advertising properties in sunny climes. The apostle who writes our verse was not the type to retire, but was often in the cold and damp for the sake of the gospel. I have reservations in a land where we shall never know cold or privation. The sun always shines for there is no night. Jesus is the light. We shall bask in Him for eternity.

—— FATHER OF LIGHTS, ——

We thank You for those who have come before us. We praise You for giving them grace to endure much for Your name's sake. Let us enter into Your rest with praises on our lips.

MOVING

For to me, to live is Christ, and to die is gain.
—Philemon 1:21

I feel sorry for young folks today. Hardly anyone builds a "starter" home anymore. But, no matter where we start on the housing ladder, our ambition is always for something better. Everyone likes a little nicer situation. The apostle Paul had assurance that his moving day would involve great gain. He was content, if God willed, to remain here, but he had to have gotten excited occasionally when he considered the great joy, and glory that awaited.

———— HEAVENLY FATHER, ————

Let our affection for this world dissolve, and cause our love for You to grow. Let us live to bear the message of Your love to others. Draw us to heaven in Your time.

WAGING THE BATTLE

Therefore, since a promise remains of entering His rest, let us fear lest any of you seem to have come short of it.

— Hebrews 4:1

The world has ever been at war. This is not because we disdain to have peace, but because each desires it upon different terms. No one wants the battle to rage forever. So we fight, that in the end, we may cease from strife. When the keening shriek of struggle grows silent, each of the victorious will have willingly submitted to God's terms. All opposition will be vanquished, and we will enter into the Lord's eternal rest.

——— PRINCE OF PEACE, ———

You have taught us that each generation must fight against evil. We stand in the stead of others who pressed, by Your command, toward victory. May that day come soon.

CHANGES

So He drove out the man; and He placed cherubim at the east of the garden of Eden, and a flaming sword which turned every way, to guard the way to the tree of life.

—Genesis 3:24

Talk about Change! Adam had dominion over the whole world. He walked in the cool of the evening with the Lord Himself. No weed intruded into his garden. Every other creature submitted to him. But then sin entered and the gates of Eden were locked behind him. We were in Adam and his failure was ours. Our ruin and death came by one man. So, also, by One came salvation and life. It was the man Christ Jesus.

——— PERFECT LORD, ———

We thank You that the richness of our salvation in Christ more than compensates that which was lost in Adam. It is all mercy and grace, and we are humbled.

CHRISTMAS REFLECTIONS

Now there were in the same country shepherds living out in the fields, keeping watch over their flock by night.

—Luke 2:8

God's ways are not man's ways. The introductions of new things to our generation are likely to be accompanied with glitter and celebrity. Certainly, the rich are first to hear, and the best and choicest will be theirs. But, God announces the birth of Messiah to the poor and lowly first. Pause and rejoice in this truth. There is no barrier of wealth or notoriety between Christ and common folk. Drink deeply from this fountain—it is free.

—— COMPASSIONATE FATHER, ——

We thank You for the freeness of Your grace. Though once poor, we are made rich. You have made us both sons and heirs.

CHRISTMAS REFLECTIONS

And she brought forth her firstborn Son, and wrapped Him in swaddling cloths, and laid Him in a manger, because there was no room for them in the inn.

—Luke 2:7

The wealth of the universe was His alone. The highest of created beings were unworthy to look upon Him. The Seraphs veiled their eyes—such was the brightness of His glory. But, look now! There is no room for Him in the world that He has made. The lowliest of beings may enter and see the Prince of Glory. We may also approach unto Christ. We may behold His beauty. His poverty has made us rich!

——— BEAUTIFUL SAVIOR, ———

We cannot imagine the condescension wherein You shed the glory that was Yours in eternity to become even as we are. Through Your poverty, we are made rich.

CHRISTMAS REFLECTIONS

And when they had come into the house, they saw the young Child with Mary His mother, and fell down and worshiped Him. And when they had opened their treasures, they presented gifts to Him: gold, frankincense, and myrrh.

—Matthew 2:11

Wise men came from the East. They were laden with rare gifts for the Christ Child. They foretold a great and awful future. Gold signified His regal lineage. Frankincense and myrrh whispered His mission. The Child had come to die! Oh, that the righteousness of His life be imputed to us. Let our sins be covered in the blood of His death. May our souls be prostrate before God in thanksgiving.

——— WONDERFUL GIFT, ———

We were Your enemies. The last thing that we might expect is this wonderful gift. It is precious beyond words, and awesome in its glory.

CHRISTMAS REFLECTIONS

Thanks be to God for His indescribable gift!
—2 Corinthians 9:15

The night of Christmas Eve is long. Anticipation lengthens each minute. Hope and joy unite to forestall the dawn. Still, though lovingly tendered, and thankfully received, earthly presents fade and decay. Consider the gift of the Father. There is no limit to His means. His vast knowledge of our need, and limitless love of our persons, inspire the perfect gift. Pause now and behold Christ. Words cannot describe Him, nor can lips utter a proper gratitude.

——— UNSPEAKABLE GIFT, ———

We thank You that eternity is long. For in this life alone we would never be able to convey our thankfulness for providing our race with the perfect gift.

Christmas Reflections

"Blessed is the Lord God of Israel, for He has visited and redeemed His people..."

—Luke 1:68

Old Zechariah had lived to see the Day of the Lord, and his heart overflowed with thanksgiving. Before the Father laid the foundation of this world, He gave an elect people to the Son. Through a long and deep night, they awaited the advent of The Redeemer. With the speaker of our verse, we rejoice that Christ is come. We need remain no longer in the darkness. Let the light of God's truth shine in your life this Christmas season.

—— Loving Father, ——

We bless Your name because You were unwilling to let our race slide into the abyss. You chose from us a people to Your name. We can never repay Your grace.

CHRISTMAS REFLECTIONS

"Glory to God in the highest, and on earth peace, goodwill toward men!"

—Luke 2:14

My father did not keep Christmas. Because of his personal convictions, he did not enter heartily into traditional celebration of the holiday. But, my memories are rich with his prayerful thanksgiving for the precious gift of God. It provoked a wonderful goodwill in him that extended to all men. He would see them all in Christ. We cannot glorify God if we neglect His great salvation. The season brings no warmth to those who stand outside His grace.

———— PRECIOUS GIFT, ————

The world will gather at this season and the season will be filled with a false mirth. There can be no Christmas without Christ. We thank You for showing Yourself to us.

CHRISTMAS REFLECTIONS

"And this will be the sign to you: You will find a Babe wrapped in swaddling cloths, lying in a manger."

—Luke 2:12

I remember when my wife and I would not erect the tree until Christmas Eve. Retail centers withheld Yule decorations until December. Now, the garish colors of Halloween are swept aside to make room for the emblems of this sacred holiday. Curiously, the "signs" of celebration are Santa Clauses, reindeer, and an assortment of cartoonish seasonal characters. We are a spiritually bankrupt generation! It seems that we would have more of Christmas, but very much less of Christ.

——— GOD OF ALL GRACE, ———

We are blessed people amid a world so dark that even the light of this season cannot penetrate it. Let us be content to brush the glitter aside, and take our portion in Christ.

NEW YEAR'S REFLECTIONS

My days are past, my purposes are broken off, even the thoughts of my heart.

—Job 17:11

This season always provokes in me a sense of my own failure and shortcomings. Some of the things that I proposed to do were left to languish because of my sloth. In others, I proposed, but God disposed. In the first instance, I repent my sluggishness, and pledge that by the grace of God, I will be more disciplined. In the latter, I yield to the Lord's sovereignty. He will work all things for my good and for His glory.

———— DEAR LORD, ————

We have labored through the heat of the day. Now the night draws on. Help us to continue in our labors as we press toward the goal.

NEW YEAR'S REFLECTIONS

For a thousand years in Your sight are like yesterday when it is past, and like a watch in the night.

—Psalms 90:4

The older I get, the more sensitive I am to the swift passage of my days. Sometimes, I find myself entering conversation with younger people. At some point, however, it will dawn on my awareness that I am not one of them. It seems but a twinkle of the eye since my hair was lush and dark, and all that hung over my belt was my tie. Those years are gone; I must prepare myself to meet my Maker.

——— DEAR LORD, ———

We have an appointment that we must keep. We must answer to our maker. Help us to prepare ourselves for that hour through repentance and good works by Your grace.

NEW YEAR'S REFLECTIONS

That which is has already been, and what is to be has already been; and God requires an account of what is past.

—Ecclesiastes 3:15

This verse is both awe inspiring and sobering. God broods over all time as though it is now. He sees yesterday and tomorrow as clearly and certainly as though it were today. I am a creature of His making, and a breather of His air. He will call me to account. It is no more than is His due. As the New Year commences, I must hold this truth before me each day. In the end, I must face God!

——— DEAR LORD, ———

We fear to stand before You. The fierceness of Your judgments will find us out. Hide us in that day in Christ. Let His merit avail for us.

NEW YEAR'S REFLECTIONS

For we have spent enough of our past lifetime in doing the will of the Gentiles-- when we walked in lewdness, lusts, drunkenness, revelries, drinking parties, and abominable idolatries.

—1 Peter 4:3

If I allow it, my past will creep in upon me and extinguish my present joy. Others seem not only to live among the yesterdays, but revel in them. Thanks be to God, we have spent enough time in the past. Let us now shake these memories from our minds. Let us dwell in our present. The Lord has saved us from what lies behind, and is in the process of fitting us for what lies before.

——— DEAR LORD, ———

Help us not to dwell on the things that cannot be recalled. Christ and heaven are before us. Let us press toward the reward that we shall have in Him.

NEW YEAR'S REFLECTIONS

Therefore we also, since we are surrounded by so great a cloud of witnesses, let us lay aside every weight, and the sin which so easily ensnares us, and let us run with endurance the race that is set before us,

—Hebrews 12:1

It is time to pick myself up. My race is not done, and there are a host of saints watching me. I am encumbered by weights from the past. Jesus can lift them from me. He has ordained good works for me to do. I must be about the things that are before me, and let go of what is past. There is no problem that I face that those who watch have not overcome. I must be up and away.

—— DEAR LORD, ——

We know that our sins were laid upon Christ. He arose from the dead in pristine purity. What then of our sins. They are gone! Help us to live in the light of that wonderful truth.

NEW YEAR'S REFLECTIONS

Then he said to them, "The Lord had better be with you when I let you and your little ones go! Beware, for evil is ahead of you."

—Exodus 10:10

I am nearer now to a land where evil does not intrude. But, I am not home yet, and I dwell in a country where dangers lurk. I know that the Lord is in control. He is my protection and my high wall. I must stay near Him. He will keep mischief from me. I must be watchful. I cannot entertain the thought that I am sufficient in myself. Without Christ, I can do nothing.

— DEAR LORD, —

We will enter the New Year with boldness because You are our protector. Help us to grasp the security that is at the center of that truth.

Author Bio:

Mr. Moore lives in Plymouth, Michigan with his wife, Jacquelynne. He is a retired business executive who has written for both newspapers and television. He is an active teacher and public speaker who writes from a deep scriptureal knowledge with a slightly antique and classic style. You may contact Mr. Moore at georgecmoore@provide.net